LISTEN!

DALE CARNEGIE
& ASSOCIATES

LISTEN!

The Art of
Effective Communication

Published by Gildan Media LLC
aka G&D Media
www.GandDmedia.com

FIRST TRADE PAPERBACK EDITION: 2019

Front Cover image: Cindy Joy

Interior design by Meghan Day Healey of Story Horse, LLC

Library of Congress Cataloging-in-Publication Data is available upon request

ISBN: 978-1-7225-1002-2

Manufactured in the United States of America by LSC Communications

10   9   8   7   6   5   4   3   2   1

The best gift you can give others
is to become a better you.
And that starts by becoming a better listener.
—JOE HART, PRESIDENT AND CEO

CONTENTS

PART THREE

You're Not Listening! Communication Breakdowns

PART FOUR

Effective Listening Techniques

FOREWORD

By Joe Hart, President and CEO of Dale Carnegie Training

Who is your "listening role model?" Although I have been blessed to know many people whom I consider to be gifted listeners, it's not an exaggeration to say that for the better part of my life, I have considered Dale Carnegie to be among my listening role models. Dale's ideas and philosophies were ever-present throughout my childhood. My parents even gave me a copy of Dale's book *How to Win Friends and Influence People.*

He is a role model to me for good reason. Dale was a trailblazer. Born into poverty on a farm in Missouri, he rose above those circumstances to become one of the most influential people of his time—and ours. My admiration for him grew as I learned more about him as a man, and as a leader. He had taken his own principles, used them to better his life, and then to change the lives of millions of others. *How to Win Friends and Influence People* is still one of the best-selling books on the market. His ideas are the foundation of Dale Carnegie Training, a global leader in personal and business development.

It was not until I took a twelve-week Dale Carnegie Training course in 1995 that Dale's ideas went from being thought-provoking to actually changing my life. Of course, a principle can't change one's life on its own. It's the *application* of those principles to our experience of the world that changes lives. I knew that in order to truly transform myself, I had to apply what I had learned in that course.

I did, and people noticed! Friends, loved ones, colleagues all started telling me that I was more confident. More friendly. I was interacting with people in a more positive way. I liked the "new me" so much that I kept learning and applying Dale Carnegie's ideas. I became such a passionate graduate of the program that I left my career to become the president and CEO of Dale Carnegie Training. Talk about changing your life!

When you change yourself, you change your life. When you change your life, you literally change the world. Not just your immediate world of your friends and colleagues. But you change THE world. Personal development can, without a doubt, change the way we interact as humans for generations to follow. I see it happen every day at work. When I travel around the world and meet with our teams, our participants, and our graduates, I see firsthand the impact that personal development is having in the world. And it makes me even more excited about the work we do.

That's why *Listen!* is such an important book. The ability to truly listen to another person is perhaps the most relevant skill you can have to change your life. It's not about what we can "get" by listening to another. It's about having a service mind-set in everything we do. Authentic listening is an opportunity to serve in its highest form.

When I first joined Dale Carnegie Training, my goal was to listen. I wanted to hear what people were saying about our company—both internally and externally. I used the concepts and principles that you'll learn in the pages that follow to truly get at the heart of what it means to be a great listener.

Of course, all personal development is an evolution. While I am a better listener now than I was a few years ago, I will be even better a few years from now. As the saying goes, "Change is the only constant. If you're not getting better, you're getting worse." It takes a passionate commitment to keep applying the principles you learn here, but once you do, you'll see your life take off in ways you can't even imagine.

As you read this book, I encourage you to think about the ideas presented and then look at where you can apply them in your life. What will becoming a better listener mean for you? How will your life change? How can you change the lives of other people? Who will look to you as their listening role model?

Have fun as you read and engage with the material. The best gift you can give others is to become a better you. And that starts by becoming a better listener.

INTRODUCTION

And so I had him thinking of me
as a good conversationalist when,
in reality, I had been merely a good listener
and had encouraged him to talk.
—DALE CARNEGIE

The Dilemma of the Orange*

Two teenagers were having an argument. They both wanted an orange, but there was only one left.

"I want it!"

"No, I do!"

Their mother heard them arguing and went to see what was going on. "How about you split it?"

They both asserted, "No! I need the whole orange."

They were devising all kinds of "fair" ways to see who would get the orange. Rock, paper, scissors. Flipping a coin. Drawing straws. But they couldn't agree on how to decide who should get the orange.

After listening to all of this, their mother said, "Well, what do you need the orange for?"

---

* This story comes from conflict management professor Dr. Alan Filley.

"I need the juice for my smoothie."

"I need the rind for my cake."

Suddenly the teenagers looked at each other and started laughing. They each could have the whole orange! One would take the juice, and the other would take the rind. It took their mother asking the right question and their listening to the answer to solve what seemed like an impossible dilemma.

The Art of Listening

How many times has this happened to you? Two people have conflicting needs, and it seems as if the only solution is that one person won't get their needs met. It happens all the time at work, at home, and in family and professional relationships.

What if there were a way to think differently? A way that smoothed conflict, built stronger relationships, and allowed you to step back and see the bigger picture? What if there were a way to make all of your relationships better? There is. It's called *listening*.

There is a way to make your relationships better. It's called listening.

Listening alone won't cut it. It's not about sitting by and passively saying, "Uh huh. And how does that make you feel?" while mentally preparing your response. You have to know the right questions to ask, how to listen effectively, and what to do once you've gained understanding.

It's about really stepping into another person's reality and seeing how they view the world.

Effective listening isn't something that comes naturally. No one is born with it. You don't see a toddler going, "So, Jimmy, what do YOU need the orange for?" Effective listening is really a learned art. After all, what is art but the practice of creation? When you actually listen to what another person is saying—not just their words, but the entire context of the communication—you create a relationship with that person. The relationship may last five minutes or fifty years. The truth is, communication creates—or destroys—relationships.

That's why Dale Carnegie Training has written this book. Although effective listening is an art, it's also a skill. Just as a painter or a sculptor masters his or her craft by learning, practicing, and repeating, you can learn to become a more effective listener. When you do, you'll find that a whole world will open up to you that you may not have seen before. A world where you can figure out what a person is really trying to say, not just what the words are conveying. One where you can manage anger and uncomfortable emotions during conversation and avoid escalating arguments. You'll discover how to listen so that the other person feels heard and is more likely to be able to hear you as well. With *Listen!,* you, too, can master the art of communication.

Listening versus Hearing

"I'm already a great listener. I can repeat back exactly what someone tells me, word for word!"

There is a huge difference between listening and hearing. Sure, you may be able to hear, and then repeat back the words someone has said. Does that mean you've *listened*? Not necessarily.

Hearing is involuntary. It's what happens when the sound vibrations of vocal expressions hit your eardrums. There probably have been many, many times when you didn't want to be hearing something, yet couldn't turn it off.

Listening involves hearing, and it also involves *understanding*. It is a participatory activity, which means you have to engage and participate in order for listening to occur. It requires concentration and awareness, so that you can take what you're hearing and give meaning to it.

We've all been in conversations where the person repeated back our exact words, yet it was clear they still didn't have a clue about what we were trying to say.

Here's an example. Two friends are sitting around talking about work. One friend works in information technology (IT), and the other does not.

The IT friend says, "It's so cool at work. We've been working on creating a new SSL VPN solution that will enhance BYOD mobility and offer seamless connectivity while securing our corporate resources. I can't wait until it's ready."

The friend who doesn't work in IT might be able to repeat back what she heard. "SSL"; "VPN"; "BYOD mobility." But unless she actually understands those terms, she has no idea what her friend is saying or what it means. And it's not only the technical terminology that matters. How does her friend feel when she is talking about this? What does the information mean to her? Just because someone is speaking and you are hearing their words doesn't mean that you're actually listening and understanding.

The "Can You Hear Me Now?" Quiz

Most people would say that they pretty good listeners. In fact, in 360-degree surveys of managers (where the manager is rated by his or her boss, peers, and direct reports), there tends to be a huge gap between the manager's self-perception as a good listener and what other people have to say.* In other words, you may THINK you're an excellent listener. Are you?

You may THINK you're an excellent listener. Are you?

To test your listening skills, take the following self-assessment quiz.

For the following questions, answer on the following scale. Try to be as honest with yourself as possible.

Not at all   Rarely   Sometimes   Often   Very often

---

* Patrick Barwise and Seán Meehan, "So You Think You're a Good Listener," Harvard Business Review, April 2008; https://hbr.org/2008/04/so-you-think-youre-a-good-listener; accessed Aug. 16, 2016.

1. When I'm on the phone with someone, it's fine to respond to e-mails and text messages at the same time as long as I'm listening.

2. When listening to another person, I start to get upset and react emotionally.

3. I feel uncomfortable with silence during conversations.

4. If I have a relevant story to share, I'll interrupt the other person in order to tell it and then get back to letting them talk.

5. People seem to get upset during some conversations with me, and it seems to come out of nowhere.

6. To keep the conversation flowing, I ask questions that can be answered with a simple "yes" or "no" response.

7. I play "devil's advocate" to help the other person see a different side of what they are saying.

8. If someone wants to talk about something over and over again, I'll just tell them what they want to hear to get them to stop.

9. As I listen, I am figuring out what I am going to say back to the other person.

10. I'm uncomfortable when people talk to me about sensitive subjects.

11. If another person has a different view on something I feel strongly about, I don't want to talk about it.

12. I don't really pay much attention to things like the environment of the conversation or body language. What matters is what the other person is actually saying.

13. If the other person is struggling to say something, I'll fill in with my own suggestions.

14. If I'm interrupted from doing something when someone wants to talk, I feel impatient for them to finish so I can get back to what I was doing.

To determine your score, give yourself the following points for each answer:

Not at all = 1 point
Rarely = 2 points
Sometimes = 3 points
Often = 4 points
Very often= 5 points

Score Interpretation

14–29: Gold Medalist

You've got terrific listening skills already. You've got the ability to make people feel heard and want to talk to you. You're emotionally present and give people your full attention. Strive to continue to grow and evolve. Keep reading this book to learn how to become an even more effective listener.

30–49: Silver Medalist

People enjoy talking to you, but sometimes if subjects get too emotional or uncomfortable, you tend to change the subject or make a joke. The tools and ideas in this book will help you continue to grow and become a more effective listener.

50–70: Bronze Medalist

If you scored in this category, you might think you're a better listener than others do. You might be giving people the feeling that you don't care about what they're saying, or you might have frequent misunderstandings. Not to worry, though. The things you'll learn in this book can certainly help you become a better listener.

The Telephone Game Model

We've probably all played the Telephone Game when we were kids. A group of kids sit in a circle, and one person whispers a sentence or phrase to the next ("The book is under the chair"), who then repeats what he or she heard by whispering it to the next person. Then the last person to hear the whisper says out loud what he or she heard ("I've got gum in my hair"). It's a funny example of how easily ideas are misinterpreted in oral communication.

Within this funny kids' game is a useful model for understanding the basics of communication. All communication involves five elements: the *sender*, the *act of encoding*, the *message*, the *act of decoding*, and the *receiver*.

The Elements of Communication

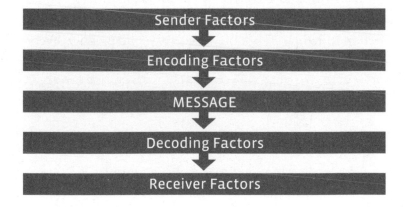

Listening is just this process in reverse. And that's how this book is arranged.

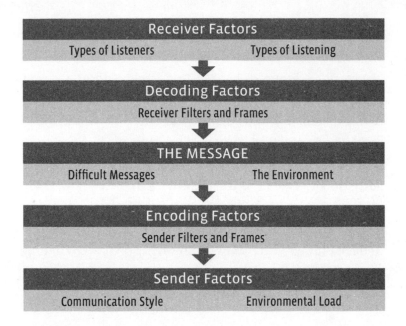

In addition, there are chapters covering communication breakdowns, and effective listening skills and techniques. At the end of the book is a comprehensive fourteen-day Better Listening Workshop, where you'll practice everything you've learned.

Are you ready to become a more effective listener? Let's get started!

The art of conversation lies in listening.
—MALCOLM FORBES

PART ONE

Receiver Factors

1. RECEIVER FRAMES AND FILTERS

*Change happens by listening and then starting
a dialogue with the people who are doing
something you don't believe is right.*
—ANTHROPOLOGIST AND
UN MESSENGER OF PEACE JANE GOODALL

One of the most famous baseball comedy acts to ever take place was the following exchange between Bud Abbott and Lou Costello. It perfectly captures how miscommunication happens when the person speaking means one thing, yet the person listening hears something different. Here's an excerpt of the exchange the duo performed on the radio.

Abbott: Well, let's see, we have on the bags, Who's on first, What's on second, I Don't Know is on third . . .

Costello: That's what I want to find out.

Abbott: I say Who's on first, What's on second, I Don't Know's on third.

Costello: Well, then, who's on first?

Abbott: Yes.

Costello: I mean the fellow's name.

Abbott: Who.

Costello: The guy on first.

Abbott: Who.

Costello: The first baseman.

Abbott: Who.

Costello: The guy playing . . .

Abbott: Who is on first!

Costello: I'm asking YOU who's on first.

Abbott: That's the man's name.

Costello: That's who's name?

Abbott: Yes.

Costello: Well, go ahead and tell me.

Abbott: That's it.

Costello: That's who?

Abbott: Yes.

The skit goes on in its hilarity, yet the point is clear. Very often the receiver hears something completely different from what the sender intended. In this case, Costello heard the word "who" as a question, whereas Abbott used the word as the name of the person on first base.

Frames

The reason we often hear things differently than the way the sender intends them to be heard has to do with what are called *frames*.

The idea of frames has been around for a very long time. In 1955, researcher Gregory Bateson said that statements "don't have intrinsic meanings, but only acquire those in a frame that is constituted by context and style."

In other words, if I make the statement, "The Denver Broncos are winning the game," the statement doesn't have any meaning at all, until the person listening has a frame for it. Where is Denver? What is a Bronco (is it the horse, or something else)? What game do they play? What does them "winning" mean to me, if anything?

If the receiver has never heard of the game of American football (or even more broadly, doesn't understand what a "game" is), does not know who the Denver Broncos are, and doesn't really care if they win or not, then the statement won't really have any meaning. The speaker might as well be stringing together a bunch of random words.

From our earliest childhood interactions with our parents and others around us, we are acquiring frames. If a child sees his dad every Sunday watching an American football game on television, he develops a frame for it. If another child, raised in another culture, sees her father watching soccer (or "football," as it is called in some countries), she will develop a frame for that. Now imagine that those two children grow up and try to have a conversation about "football," but they both have completely different frames for what that word means. It could be Abbott and Costello all over again.

---

*Your frame is your broad understanding
of a situation or topic.*

A frame is, in essence, a broad "macro" view of a given situation. It's as if your mind were unconsciously looking at things through a camera lens. It puts some things in and leaves other things out. A receiver can only hear or receive things that enter through the frame. And our frames are influenced by our gender, education, assumptions, personal agenda, sense of efficacy, relationship with the other person, and more. The experiences we have in the world, the things we learn and observe, all lead to frames.

The thing is, our frame is very often unconscious, meaning that we aren't always aware of how our experiences are shaping our perceptions.

Here's a clever joke that illustrates how the unconscious frame of language can affect a conversation.

A woman goes into her lawyer's office requesting a divorce. He is taking her background information and asks her, "Do you have grounds for a divorce?"

To which she replies, "Well, we have three acres."

"No, ma'am. What I mean is, does he beat you up?" asks the attorney.

"No, I get up around 6:30 and he sleeps until 7:00," she responds.

Feeling a little frustrated, the attorney asks, "Lady, tell me, do you have a grudge?"

Looking very confident, she states, "No, we have a carport."

At this point the lawyer has lost his patience and asks, "Look, lady. Why the heck do you want a divorce?"

"Because he never listens!"

In this joke, the attorney is using a legal frame for his questions. The woman hears the words "grounds," "beat you up," and "grudge" differently because of her frame.

Frames Can Lead to Bias

Unconscious frames can lead to bias as well. You can see it on social media all the time. A flash of light streaks across the sky, and people's frames determine what they believe is the cause. Some people think it's a UFO and the government is covering up evidence. Others believe that it is a sign from God that the apocalypse is near. Still others see it as a scientific event in which a gaseous meteor entered the atmosphere. In each case, the person's frame is influencing what they believe and how they interpret the event.

How often have you had it happen where you hear something and automatically assume that it means one thing, and then you get some information that totally shifts your frame? For example, you hear your mate whispering on the phone, giving details about meeting somewhere. Depending on your frame, you might assume that your mate is planning on meeting a lover. But if you remember that your birthday is a week away, that might shift your frame to make you assume that your mate is planning some kind of surprise for you.

Let's try a little exercise. What is the first interpretation that comes to mind when you hear the following things?

- "Have you eaten yet?"
- "Oh, I'm sorry you didn't like the movie."
- "Where would you like to go to dinner?"

Here are some different frames for how those statements can be interpreted.

"Have you eaten yet?"

This question could be taken as an invitation to share a meal ("Then come on over for dinner!"), a criticism for one's eating habits ("It's 3:00 p.m.!"), or a factual inquiry about the person's food consumption.

"Oh, I'm sorry you didn't like the movie."

This statement could be taken as an apology for choosing a movie the person didn't like ("I never should have made you watch a chick flick"), a hostile comment on the person's taste in movies ("You never like the same movies I like"), or a neutral acknowledgement that the other person didn't like the movie.

"Where would you like to go to dinner?"

This question is a classic argument-starter in many relationships. The question can be received as "Tell me where you want to go to dinner and we'll go there." Or it can be framed as a setup for potential conflict, if the receiver answers the question and the sender doesn't like the choice the receiver makes. "How about we go to Ned's?" "We went to Ned's yesterday!" Or it can be framed as the beginning of a dialogue.

It's easy to see from these three examples how a person's frame influences how he or she hears—and responds to—another person's words. It's also easy to see how the different variables—gender, education, your relationship and history with the other person, etc.—play into these kinds of situations. If you have repeated experiences with someone, it tends to create a frame through which you then see ALL of your interactions with that person.

If you have a conflict-filled relationship with your mother, and she asks, "Have you eaten yet?", you are more likely to see that as a critical statement. If your romantic partner says, "Have you eaten yet?", you're more likely to see the question as an invitation to share a meal. Same words, totally different interpretation.

If you have repeated experiences with someone, it tends to create a frame through which you then see ALL of your interactions with that person.

Filters

Does this mean that we are all doomed to receive information from these often unconscious frames and then act on our biased information? No, not at all. There is another element that factors into how we receive information. They are called *filters*.

While a frame is a "big picture" view of a situation, a filter is a conscious choice to focus more on one thing than another. Using the photography analogy, the frame is what the camera lens can see. The filter is what it chooses to focus on—what areas are sharp and what are blurry, what areas are light and which are darkened?

Our filters are the way we can change how we receive what someone is saying. It's important to note that a filter is not a good thing or a bad thing. It's simply a way of managing all of the data that come into our minds.

The Window Example

Here's a great illustration of how filters can affect perception. Two people walk into a room with a huge glass window that looks out onto a 180-degree panoramic ocean view.

Mary says, "Look at that view of the ocean!"

Bill says, "I can barely see out the window, with all the dirt on it. Someone should really clean it."

Mary replies, "Can you imagine seeing the sun streaming in like this every morning when you wake up?"

Bill answers, "I can imagine that it would be too bright

in the morning. And where is the privacy? I would definitely need curtains."

Mary in this instance is focusing on what is outside the window—the ocean, the sunlight streaming in. Bill is focusing on the window itself. Mary has a positive view of the window, because she is filtering out the dirty window and the lack of privacy. Bill has a negative view of the window, because he is filtering out the beautiful view. Instead he is focusing on the need for curtains, the need for clean windows, and the lack of privacy.

It's not that one person is right and the other is wrong. The view IS beautiful. And the window is dirty. It is in this moment in the interaction, though, that the two people can choose to step back and look at how the other person's frames and filters affect their perception, or can escalate it to an argument.

Here are two possible outcomes from that conversation.

Outcome One

"Look at that view of the ocean!" says Mary.

"I can barely see out the window, with all the dirt on it. Someone should really clean it," Bill replies.

"Can you imagine seeing the sun streaming in like this every morning when you wake up?" Mary says.

"I can imagine that it would be too bright in the morning. And where is the privacy? I would definitely need curtains," Bill says.

"You are always so negative. How come you can't ever appreciate the beauty in a situation? All you ever do is criticize!" Mary replies.

"Well, somebody has to be realistic. After all, are you the one who has to clean the windows? No. That's my chore. And you may not care if the whole neighborhood sees you undressed. I do!" Bill shouts back.

Outcome Two

"Look at that view of the ocean!" says Mary.

"I can barely see out the window, with all the dirt on it. Someone should really clean it," Bill replies.

"Can you imagine seeing the sun streaming in like this every morning when you wake up?" Mary says.

"I can imagine that it would be too bright in the morning. And where is the privacy? I would definitely need curtains," Bill says.

"I bet this window reminds you of when you were a kid and your mom made you clean the sliding glass doors over and over again until they were spotless," Mary says warmly.

"It sure does! Not to mention my nosy neighbors looking in at us all the time. The view sure is pretty. Reminds me of our honeymoon," responds Bill.

In Outcome One, both Mary and Bill got frustrated with the other person for not having the same filter as they did. In Outcome Two, the couple each consciously chose to listen to the other person's statements and tried to determine how and why their filters differed.

Effective listening comes from understanding your own frames and filters and how they influence how you receive the other person's message.

Emotional Control

Choosing to identify our own filters and those of others requires that we maintain a certain level of control over our emotions when we are listening to the other person. It's easy to listen to someone who has the same frame and is using the same filters as you are. It becomes increasingly difficult when you're conversing with someone who sees the world completely different from you.

Conflict researchers Roger Fisher and William Ury, in their classic text *Getting to Yes,* mention several techniques for managing emotions during conflict. Strong emotions are both a cause and a result of conflict. People in conflict may have a variety of negative emotions—anger, distrust, disappointment, frustration, confusion, worry, or fear. Here are some tips, based on Fisher and Ury's work, for managing those strong emotions.

1. When you feel yourself getting emotional, step back and focus on what the other person's emotions are. Are they angry or just excited and passionate about the subject?

2. Look to find the source of the emotions. What are their filters in the situation that could be causing

their feelings and actions? Is it possible that the filter has nothing to do with you?

3. Talk about the other person's feelings openly. "It seems like this conversation is making you angry. Am I misreading it?"

4. Express your own feelings in a nonconfrontational way (using "I" statements instead of "you" statements). "I suppose I am feeling angry because . . ."

5. Validate the other person's feelings and their right to see something differently than you do.

6. If the other person isn't able to step back from their emotions, then you be the one to do it. Don't react emotionally; instead step out of the room and give both people a chance to calm down.

Here's an example of how that might look in action.

Susan and Tim are co-chairing a charity event at work. Susan has the frame that co-chairs should share all of the information openly, and have frequent conversations about the project.

Tim, on the other hand, has the frame that each of them has a complementary role and that each person should be responsible simply for doing their own part, and then letting the other person know. Because of this, he's less communicative with Susan than she is comfortable with.

The result is that Susan becomes more aggressive in her attempts to communicate with Tim. She begins e-mailing him daily, sending him text messages, and asking other people if they know what is going on. "He's not responding to me! How can we run this event together if I don't even know what he's doing?"

Tim's response to this is to back off even further and to stop replying to her messages and calls. "She's micromanaging me! How am I supposed to get anything done with her breathing down my neck?"

To solve this, Tim and Susan can use the six tips given above.

1. Step back and focus on the other person's emotions. Susan could see that Tim is frustrated. Tim could see that Susan is in a panic.

2. Look to find the source of the emotions. The two people have different frames and are focusing on different things. Tim might see that Susan's frame is that "we are doing this together." This causes her to focus on the volume of communication. If she's not hearing from him enough, she'll feel anxious. Susan might see that Tim's frame is, "Let's divide up the tasks and each of us do our part." This causes him to focus on the tasks and their completion, rather than on the volume of information. She might see that his frustration comes from her not focusing on the work that needs to be done.

3. Talk about their feelings openly. "I get the sense that you're frustrated with how this project is going."

4. Express their feelings in a nonconfrontational way. "I just get stressed out when I don't know if things are getting done or not." "I feel pressured when you ask me all the time how things are going."

5. Validate the other person's feelings. "I can see why you're anxious when you don't know how my part of the project is coming along." "And I can see why you feel pressured when I'm calling and writing all the time."

6. Step out of the room if need be. "Let's hold this conversation for ten minutes. I need a drink of water."

This chapter has focused on the receiver's frames and filters and how they affect listening. Chapter two goes into more depth about the different types of listeners, and about how these frames and filters can become habitual personality characteristics.

2. THE SEVEN TYPES OF LISTENERS

You can make more friends in two months
by becoming interested in other people
than you can in two years by trying to get
other people interested in you.
—DALE CARNEGIE

Dr. Porter was lecturing to his college freshman business psychology class one afternoon when he began to suspect that they weren't really listening to him. He was outlining his classic theory of motivation and decided to ask them some questions to shake things up.

Brad looked as if he would rather be elsewhere. He was sitting there, tapping his foot, watching the clock, and checking his phone every minute or so. "Mr. Lawson, this model says that the value of a reward is part of what motivates a person's behavior. Would you agree?"

"Uhh, yeah. Sure." Brad answered, never taking his eyes off his phone.

Melanie was sitting at her desk and just staring off into space. Dr. Porter walked over to the window that she was gazing out of and stood directly in her line of sight. "Ms.

Griffin, the next element of the model says that motivation is influenced by the amount of effort spent. What do you think about that?"

Being spoken to shocked Melanie out of her daydream. "What? I'm sorry, I didn't hear you."

"What I was saying," Dr. Porter continued, "is that motivation is a factor of several things. Whether the reward is valuable, the eff . . ."

Suddenly Breanna interrupted. "It's the effort spent and the probability of getting the reward." She leaned back and smiled.

Dr. Porter then asked the girl next to her, "Ms. Brenner, what do you find rewarding enough to expend effort for?"

Caitlyn just looked blankly at him through her thickly made up eyelashes. "Nothing."

Next to her, Danny mumbled, "No wonder. You emo types don't care about anything."

Dr. Porter walked over to Danny's desk. "Well, then, Mr. Valdez, what do you find rewarding?"

"Sleep. Because that's what this class makes me feel like doing."

Then Gene piped in. "What seems to be going on here, actually, is that Breanna finds it intrinsically rewarding to demonstrate her knowledge in class, yet also believes that if the professor is aware of her understanding she will earn a better grade in the class. Danny, on the other hand, doesn't feel that he has the ability to succeed in the class, so he masks it with an attitude of hostility."

In the back row of the class was a quiet girl, Anna. She shyly raised her hand. "Dr. Porter? You created this model with your colleague Dr. Lawler, right? How did you come to expand on the classic Vroom expectancy theory?"

Dr. Porter smiled and walked back to the front of the room. At least *someone* was listening. "That's right, Ms. Patel. Ed and I took Victor Vroom's theory of expectancy and introduced additional aspects to it. Let's look at this diagram . . ."

Seven Types of Listeners

How many times have you been talking and encountered someone like the students in Dr. Porter's class? How many times have you actually *been* one of those listeners?

The above scenario illustrates the seven types of listeners identified by Dale Carnegie Training.

The "Preoccupieds"
The "Out-to-Lunchers"
The "Interrupters"
The "Whatevers"
The "Combatives"
The "Analysts"
The "Engagers"

The first six types are less effective than the seventh. Here is a more in-depth description of each of the types.

The "Preoccupieds"

Brad was a classic "Preoccupied." Tapping his foot and looking at the clock gives the speaker the impression that he isn't giving his full attention. These people come across as rushed and are constantly looking around or doing something else. Also known as "Multitaskers," these people cannot sit still and listen.

The "Out-to-Lunchers"

In the above scenario, Melanie was an "Out-to-Luncher." Dr. Porter was talking, but she was daydreaming instead of listening. These people are physically there for you, but mentally they are not. You can tell this by the blank look on their faces. They are either daydreaming or thinking about something else entirely.

The "Interrupters"

Breanna is an "Interrupter." She was just waiting for her chance to jump in and speak. These people are ready to chime in at any given time. They are perched and ready for a break to complete your sentence for you. They are not listening to you. They are focused on trying to guess what you will say and what they want to say.

The "Whatevers"

Caitlyn is a classic "Whatever." Even if she isn't actually using the word, her body language and demeanor gave Dr. Porter the feeling she didn't care about what he was saying at all. These people remain aloof and show little emotion when listening. They do not seem to care about anything you have to say.

The "Combatives"

It's pretty clear that Danny was a "Combative." Hostile and rude, the Combative listener isn't listening for understanding. He or she is listening to get ammunition to use against you. These people are armed and ready for war. They enjoy disagreeing and blaming others.

The "Analysts"

Gene is an "Analyst." He probably has no idea that his listening style is ineffective. These people are constantly in the role of counselor or therapist, and they are ready to provide you with unsolicited answers. They think they are great listeners and love to help. They are constantly in an analyze-what-you-are-saying-and-fix-it mode.

The "Engagers"

Finally, Anna is an example of an "Engager." These are the consciously aware listeners. They listen with their eyes, ears, and hearts and try to put themselves in the speaker's shoes. This is listening at the highest level. Their listening skills encourage you to continue talking, discover your own solutions, and let your ideas unfold.

No one can be an engaged listener all the time.

Can You Hear Me Now?

Although it can be challenging to try and communicate with several of these types, there are some things you can do to get through to them. Here are some tips on how to speak to each of the types.

The "Preoccupieds"

If you are speaking to a "Preoccupied" listener, you might ask, "Is this a good time?" or say, "I need your undivided attention for just a moment." Begin with a statement that will get their attention, be brief, and get to the bottom line quickly, because their attention span is short.

The "Out-to-Lunchers"

If you are speaking to an "Out-to-Luncher," check in with them every now and again and ask if they've understood what you were saying. As with the "Preoccupieds," begin with a statement that will catch their attention. Be concise and to the point, because their attention span is also short.

The "Interrupters"

If you are speaking to an "Interrupter," when they chime in, stop immediately and let them talk, or they will never listen to you. When they are done, you might acknowledge their comment and then say, "As I was saying before . . ." to bring their interruption to their attention.

The "Whatevers"

If you are speaking to a "Whatever," dramatize your ideas and ask your listener questions to maintain their involvement.

The "Combatives"

If you are speaking to a "Combative," when he or she disagrees or points the blame, look forward instead of back. Talk about how you might agree to disagree or about what can be done differently next time.

The "Analysts"

If you are speaking to an "Analyst," you might begin by saying, "I just need to run something by you. I'm not looking for any advice."

The "Engagers"

If you are speaking to an "Engager," take the time to acknowledge their attentiveness. Thank them for their interest in you and your topic.

What If It's *You*?

Perhaps you recognized yourself in one or more of the types. No need to worry at all! No one is an "Engager" all of the time. Here are some tips for what to do if you catch yourself in one of the less effective listening types.

The "Preoccupieds"

If you are a "Preoccupied" listener, make a point to set aside what you are doing when someone is speaking to you.

The "Out-to-Lunchers"

If you are an "Out-to-Luncher," act like a good listener. Be alert, maintain eye contact, lean forward, and show interest by asking questions.

The "Interrupters"
If you are an "Interrupter," make a point to apologize every time you catch yourself interrupting. This will make you more conscious of it.

The "Whatevers"
If you are a "Whatever," concentrate on the full message, not just on the verbal message. Make a point to listen with your eyes, ears, and heart. Pay attention to body language and try to understand why this person wants to talk to you about this issue.

The "Combatives"
If you are a "Combative," make an effort to put yourself in the speaker's shoes and understand, accept, and find merit in the other's point of view.

The "Analysts"
If you are an "Analyst," relax and understand that not everyone is looking for an answer, solution, or advice. Some people just like bouncing ideas off other people because it helps them see the answers more clearly themselves.

The "Engagers"
If you are an "Engager," keep it up. People truly appreciate this about you.

As we've mentioned, no one can be an engaged listener all of the time. In fact, we all vary from being attentive to what is being said, being selective in our focus, and being distracted over time. Here's a visual illustration.

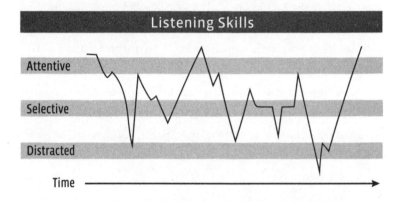

How much time we spend being attentive, selective, and distracted can vary depending on a lot of factors. We will get into many of these in later chapters.

How much time we spend being attentive, selective, and distracted can vary.

Two Types of Distractions

According to Daniel Goleman, author of *Focus: The Hidden Power of Excellence*, distractions come in two main kinds, *sensory distractions* (things happening around you) and *emotional distractions* (your inner dialogue, thoughts about things happening in your life).

When you are listening to someone speak and find your mind wandering off, you can check in and ask yourself, "What is distracting me? Is it a sensory distraction or an emotional distraction?" By identifying the fact that you are distracted, you can then shift your focus (using the idea of filters, as discussed in chapter one) to become more selective in what you are attending to. You might think, "That beeping sound is annoying, so I'm going to focus on what she is saying instead." Or, "My mind keeps wandering back to that argument I had with my boss this afternoon. I need to focus on what he is telling me about his day."

In this chapter, we've talked about the seven different types of listeners and have discovered some tips for communicating with them, and avoiding being some of them! In chapter three, we'll get into the four types of listening.

3. THE FOUR TYPES OF LISTENING

Most people do not listen with the intent to understand; they listen with the intent to reply.
—STEPHEN R. COVEY

When a man whose marriage was in trouble sought his advice, the Master said, "You must learn to listen to your wife."

The man took this advice to heart and returned after a month to say he had learned to listen to every word his wife was saying.

Said the Master with a smile, "Now go home and listen to every word she *isn't* saying."

We've all done it at one time or another—not really listened to someone. Maybe you were preoccupied with something else. Maybe you weren't interested in the topic. Or maybe you thought you were listening when you weren't. In this chapter we'll cover four types of listening. They are: *Pretending to Listen, Listening to Prepare Your Response, Listening to Learn*, and *Listening for Empathy*.

Of course, this isn't the ultimate list of listening types. A quick Internet search can reveal numerous other labels and descriptions of different types of listening. But these four types can encompass the others.

To best experience the different types, let's take a look at them in action. The listener's thoughts appear in parentheses next to the dialogue.

Leah's Lecture

Leah is like many sixteen-year old girls. She's not very good at keeping her room clean. One day her dad comes in and begins to lecture her on the merits of cleanliness.

"Leah, how many times have I told you not to leave food and dirty dishes in your room? Don't you remember last summer when we had that ant problem? We had to fumigate the entire house! That cost me . . ."

"Sorry, Dad." (*Maybe if I apologize he'll stop talking . . . no . . . he's not stopping. I already know what he's going to say, so I'm not going to listen.*)

"And then, after the fumigation was over, we had to wash every dish in the house . . ."

(*I wonder what Breanna is doing? I bet she texted me. I wish Dad would just stop talking so I can check my phone. He's just going on and on and on!*)

"So that's why I tell you that you can't leave food and dishes in your room."

What Leah is doing in this scene is the type of listening called *Pretending to Listen*. Also called *False Listening*, this is when the listener is giving the impression that he or she is listening, yet is really daydreaming or thinking about something else.

People tend to engage in this type of "listening" when they are bored with, or don't want to hear, what the other person is saying. There are circumstances where it's not acceptable to just say, "I am not listening to you." A power differential like that between a parent and a child can create one of those circumstances.

Pretending to Listen is when the listener is giving the impression that he or she is listening, yet is really daydreaming or thinking about something else.

Terry and the Tirade

Terry's manager, Carol, comes into her office just before lunch and asks her about a sales report she is almost finished with. Terry has received some incorrect figures and needs to revise the report before giving it to the regional sales manager.

"Why haven't you given the report to Brian yet? I saw it come in two hours ago."

(*The reason I haven't given it to him is that I don't want to give incorrect sales figures. The last time I did that you yelled at me for half an hour.*)

"I just don't understand what the delay is. Brian is only in town for one day, and this is a rush project. He needs to have time to read it and ask questions before he flies out tonight."

(*Should I tell her about the incorrect sales figures? That would get me out of trouble, but it might freak her out, and then she'll want to go over the whole report with me. Maybe I can just make the changes and get it on her desk before lunch.*)

"Sorry about that, Carol. I'm just proofing the report. I'll print it and get it on your desk before lunch."

What Terry is doing here is called *Listening to Prepare Your Response*. This is when you only listen to what is being said so that you can explain or defend your position. While you may be partially listening to what is being said, you are filtering out anything that won't help you in your response.

Listening to Prepare Your Response is when you only listen in order to explain or defend your position.

Sophia in Spanish

Sophia has been waiting for this Spanish-language class ever since her sister gave her a gift certificate for it on her birthday. She's planning on taking a trip to Mexico next summer and wants to learn to speak the language before she goes.

On the first day of class, Sophia arrives, takes a seat in front, and gets out her notebook. The instructor, Rogelio, walks in.

"*Hola, mi nombre es Rogelio,*" he says. "That means, 'Hello, my name is Rogelio' in Spanish."

Lucy writes that down. "*Hola* means 'hello.' *Mi nombre* means 'my name'."

"Now let's learn how to say 'good morning,' 'good afternoon,' and 'goodnight.' *Buenos dias. Buenas tardes. Y buenos noches.*"

Sophia writes that down and thinks, "I better pay close attention in this class if I want to learn Spanish by summer."

Sophia is doing what is called *Listening to Learn*. It's a type of listening, but one that is highly selective. She's not listening to determine how Rogelio feels or to place herself in his shoes. She is listening to gather information.

Listening to Learn is selectively filtering out everything except the information desired.

Caring Casey

Casey is the human resources director at a video production company. It's time for performance evaluations, which is her least favorite time of year. One by one she calls various employees into her office to give them feedback about their work performance.

First up is Marcus. His peers have been telling Casey that he tends to doze off in his cubicle in the afternoons.

"Hi Marcus, come on in. Have a seat."

He looks a little nervous. "Thanks, Casey."

"So tell me what's going on. I hear you've been feeling a little tired lately." (*He actually looks exhausted!*)

"Yeah, it's been rough. My wife's car died and we are down to sharing a car. She has to drop the kids off at day care and school before she goes to work, and her job is twenty miles from our house. So I've been letting her take the car. I mean, that's what a man does, right?"

(*He seems like a really nice guy . . .*)

"So anyway, our house is still ten miles from here, and I have to walk the first three miles before the buses start running in order to make it here on time. I can catch a bus on Sixth Street, but I still have to leave the house at 4:30 a.m. to get to work. So by 3:00 p.m., I am really dragging."

(*How awful! And yet he's hardly ever late to work. I wonder if there is something we can do.*)

"Did you know that Kevin lives over by you? Maybe he'd be willing to pick you up?"

(*That sure perked him up.*)

"Oh man, that would be awesome. I had no idea. I'll ask him at my lunch break. Thank you so much!"

What Casey is doing is demonstrating *Listening for Empathy*. Also known as *Whole Person Listening*, it's seeking to understand the person, their personality, and their real and unspoken meanings and motivators.

**Listening for Empathy is seeking
to understand the whole person.**

This chapter has briefly covered the four types of listening, and is the end of part one of the book—Receiver Factors. But before we move on to part two, Sender Factors, let's apply what you've learned in a section called *My Listening Log*. In this section, you'll have the opportunity to interact with the ideas presented in the first three chapters of the book. We recommend that you use a journal or notebook so that you can track your progress as you learn to become a better listener.

My Listening Log, Part One

Frames

Your frame is your broad understanding of a situation or topic.

---

1. On another piece of paper or a journal, answer this question: "What are some of the frames I learned about the topic of listening?" Here are some examples.

   Children should be seen and not heard.
   You're given two ears and one mouth for a reason.
   In our family, you had to shout in order to be heard.
   No one listens to me anyway, so I might as well not try.
   I say the stupidest things.

2. What biases do your frames lead to? Do you, or does someone you know, have an unconscious frame that gets in the way of effective communication? Write down these biases in your journal.

3. What role do you think gender, education, religion, race, and similar factors have in how a person listens?

Filters

A filter is a conscious choice to focus more on one thing than another.

What are some filters you use when listening to the following people? In other words, what information do you focus on the most when communicating with the person, and what do you leave out?

1. Your parents
2. Your significant other
3. Your children
4. Your boss
5. Clients or customers
6. Your best friend

Now shift the filter a little. What is something unusual or different you could listen for when communicating with those people? Example: looking at your parents as a husband and wife to each other.

1. Your parents
2. Your significant other
3. Your children
4. Your boss
5. Clients or customers
6. Your best friend

Emotional Control

In your journal, describe an instance where you could have done a better job controlling your emotions during a conflict.

Then apply the six steps to identify what you could have done differently.

1. Step back and focus on the other person's emotions.

2. Look to find the source of the emotions. Is it the result of different frames or filters?

3. Talk about feelings openly.

4. Express feelings in a nonconfrontational way.

5. Validate the other person's feelings.

6. Step out of the room if need be.

Seven Types of Listeners

Identify people in your life who represent the seven types of listeners.

The "Preoccupieds"
The "Out-to-Lunchers"
The "Interrupters"
The "Whatevers"
The "Combatives"
The "Analysts"
The "Engagers"

Identify times when *you* were each of these seven types.

Two Types of Distractions

Describe a time when you were listening and your mind wandered off. Was it a sensory distraction or an emotional distraction? Try to come up with examples of each.

Four Types of Listening

For each of the four types, identify someone in your life who engages in that type of listening frequently.

Pretending to Listen
Listening to Prepare Your Response
Listening to Learn
Listening for Empathy

Now for each of the four types, identify an instance in which *you* engaged in that type of listening.

The art of conversation lies in listening.
—MALCOM FORBES

PART TWO

Sender Factors

4. SENDER FILTERS AND FRAMES

It's important to be precise about words, because of the thought value of them— they frame and shape so much of the way we understand things.
—MICHAEL NESMITH

Frame One

Once upon a time, at the edge of a big forest, a little girl lived with her mother. She always wore a red hat and cape and was called Little Red Riding Hood.

One day Little Red Riding Hood's mother gave her a basket and told her to walk through the forest to the other side, where her grandmother lay sick in bed.

"Remember not to talk to strangers," Little Red Riding Hood's mother warned.

On the way to her grandmother's house, Little Red Riding Hood met the Big Bad Wolf.

"Where are you going, little girl?" he asked with his biggest smile.

"To my grandmother's house on the other side of the forest," said Little Red Riding Hood, who had forgotten her mother's warning.

The wolf ran off, taking a shortcut ahead to Grandmother's house. When he got there, he went inside and swallowed Grandmother whole! He then put on her cap and nightgown and climbed into bed.

When Little Red Riding Hood got there, she walked right up to the bed.

"Grandmother, what big ears you have!" she said.

"All the better to hear you with, my dear," said the wolf.

"And what big eyes you have!" said Little Red Riding Hood.

"All the better to see you with, my dear," said the wolf.

"And what huge teeth you have!" the little girl exclaimed.

"All the better to eat you with!" said the wolf as he jumped out of bed and started chasing Little Red Riding Hood.

A woodsman who was chopping wood nearby heard Little Red Riding Hood screaming. He came inside and hit the wolf over the head with his ax. The wolf fell to the ground, and out popped Grandmother, safe and sound.

Then the woodsman, Little Red Riding Hood, and Grandmother all had cake and tea.

Frame Two

Once upon a time, at the edge of a big forest, lived a friendly wolf. Because he was so scary looking, he had no friends. The forest creatures called him the Big Bad Wolf. But he was not bad, just shy.

Down the creek from the wolf's house lived a little girl lived with her mother. She always wore a red hat and cape and was called Little Red Riding Hood.

While Little Red Riding Hood's mother was a very nice woman, she had an evil grandmother who lived on the other side of the forest. The wolf had heard say in the forest that she planned to kill Little Red Riding Hood the next time she came to visit.

One day Little Red Riding Hood's mother gave her a basket and told her to walk through the forest to the other side, where her grandmother lay sick in bed.

"She may be evil, but we must be nice to her anyway, for she is family," Little Red Riding Hood's mother said.

On the way to her grandmother's house, Little Red Riding Hood met the Big Bad Wolf.

"Where are you going, little girl?" he asked with his biggest smile.

"To my grandmother's house on the other side of the forest," said Little Red Riding Hood.

Worried for Little Red Riding Hood's safety, the wolf ran off, taking a shortcut ahead to Grandmother's house. When he got there, he went inside and swallowed Grandmother whole! He then put on her cap and nightgown and climbed into bed.

When Little Red Riding Hood got there, she walked right up to the bed.

"Grandmother, what big ears you have!" she said.

"All the better to hear you with, my dear," said the wolf.

"And what big eyes you have," said Little Red Riding Hood.

"All the better to see you with, my dear," said the wolf.

"And what huge teeth you have!" the little girl exclaimed.

"All the better to eat with you!" said the wolf as he jumped out of bed, to go share some cake and tea now that he had saved Little Red Riding Hood from her evil grandmother.

Little Red Riding Hood did not know the wolf had saved her from certain death at the hands of her evil grandmother, and so she screamed and ran away.

A woodsman who was chopping wood nearby heard Little Red Riding Hood screaming. He came inside and hit the wolf over the head with his ax. The wolf fell to the ground, and out popped Grandmother. She was so angry that she took the ax and killed everyone, and then ate the cake and tea herself.

These two stories, each written from a different frame, perfectly illustrate the idea that the sender's frames can influence the listener's perceptions of what is being said.

In both versions of the story, the facts are the same, at least initially. Little Red Riding Hood takes a basket across the forest to her grandmother's house, meeting the wolf along the way. The wolf beats her to Grandmother's house, eats Grandmother, and gets bonked over the head by the woodsman as he is chasing Little Red Riding Hood.

The meaning of the story varies depending on the additional information we are given. In the first version, the wolf is framed as the bad guy: he eats an old grandmother and chases Little Red Riding Hood. In the second version, the reader is given a piece of information not present in the first version—the grandmother is evil! The wolf is trying to *save* Little Red Riding Hood, not eat her! This slight shift in frame lends a completely different meaning to the facts of the story.

Sender Frames Bias Listeners

The same thing happens in conversations every day, all day long. Most often senders aren't *intentionally* trying to frame things to bias the view of the listener—although often enough they are. (One area where this happens quite a bit is in the television news industry.)

In 1993, researcher Robert Entman wrote, "To frame is to select some aspects of a perceived reality and make them more salient in a communicating text, in such a way as to promote a particular problem definition, causal interpretation, moral evaluation, and/or treatment recommendation." In other words, framing is taking some part of the story and communicating it in a way that emphasizes one thing over another in order to make your point.

We've all seen it. One channel shows a political candidate looking handsome or pretty and kissing babies. The other channel shows that same candidate frowning and angrily yelling at someone. One frame gives a positive impression of the candidate; the other gives a negative impression. Same candidate, different images, depending on how the information is presented.

Linguist Deborah Tannen has spent her career studying and writing about communication style differences and what influences the way we talk—and about the way we hear things. In her book *Talking from 9 to 5: Women and Men at Work*, she says that "our ways of talking are influenced by every aspect of our communities, so no two women or no two men are exactly alike, any more than any two New Yorkers or Spaniards or forty-year-olds are alike. Yet understanding the patterns of influence on our styles is crucial to understanding what happens to us in our conversations—and our lives."

For example, if you see someone you know, you're likely to ask, "How are you?", chat, and then go your separate ways. Most of us never really stop to think about how those interactions are shaped by factors such as gender, culture, language, and age. An American is likely to extend his or her hand for a handshake, whereas a Japanese person might bow. Two women might kiss each other's cheeks or embrace, and that would be socially acceptable. Two men doing the same thing might be acceptable or not, depending on the country they're in.

People of similar backgrounds—gender, education, age, country of origin, etc.— tend to have similar frames about things.

The Conversation Sandwich

Here's an example of how the similarities and differences between sender and receiver can affect their interactions.

Mike and Mary have both completed quarterly summary reports at work. Their boss, Don, wants each of them to make some revisions on the report. First he calls Mary in.

Being a fairly direct communicator, he gets right to the point. "Mary: About that report. I need to see some of last month's figures on page eleven. And the font you used is too small. Use a bigger one. OK? And have the revisions in my inbox by Friday."

Mary leaves his office in tears, thinking, *I can't believe what a jerk he is. All he did was criticize the report. He always acts like he has it out for me. Did he even notice the embedded hyperlinks to the monthly sales reports? And that font isn't too small. Everyone else could read it just fine!*

Don sees how upset Mary was at his comments. Not wanting to be seen as a mean boss, he changes things up when Mike comes in.

"Mike, hi, have a seat. So, first of all, thank you *so* much for getting that report to me on time. You have no idea how much pressure I've been under from management to turn those things in. Your report looks good. There were a couple of things I would have liked to see differently. It would have been great if you could have included some of last month's sales figures on page eleven. And maybe used a bigger font. But overall, you did a good job on the report."

Mike leaves thinking, *Hey, I did a good job on that report! Don did suggest things for me to do differently next time. But he said the report was fine.* Mike never heard that he actually needed to make any changes, so he won't make them.

Friday comes and goes, and neither Mary nor Mike turn in the revisions. Mary doesn't turn them in because she was so overwhelmed by Don's criticism that she stopped listening. Mike didn't turn them in because Don wasn't direct enough in stating that he actually expected Mike to make the revisions. All Mike heard was, "Thank you for the report, looks good, blah blah blah, good job."

And now Don is angry that neither of them did what he thought he asked them to do. He begins to attribute it to their characters. "Mary is so hypersensitive! And, Mike, well, he's just lazy and arrogant."

What started out as a simple communication error has now blown up into a serious workplace issue.

The problem was that Don did not match his communication style to the style of the person he was talking to. Although he has a naturally direct style of communication (based on his gender, his background, and his personal style), it's not a match to Mary's indirect style.

If he had used the "conversation sandwich" with Mary—giving a compliment, a criticism, and then a compliment, as he did with Mike, Mary would have been able to hear the criticism in a way that she could understand.

Similarly, because Mike is a direct communicator like Don, Don needed to get right to the point, as he did with Mary: "This is what I need, and this is when I need it."

How to Listen for Frames

Of course this is a book on listening, not on talking. And while they are interconnected, the perspective of this book is from that of the listener.

So what are some things the listener can do to become a more effective listener, no matter who is speaking? One thing is to try and identify the frame and other factors that are affecting the way the speaker is speaking.

For example, in our example above, Mary made an assumption about Don's intent that was flawed. Because the only parts of the report that Don pointed out were the things he wanted changed, she took his comments as critical and then generalized that he is a "jerk" who had it out for her.

Instead Mary might have stepped back and asked, "What's another way to frame this? I'm assuming that Don is just being a jerk and overly critical. But if that weren't true, then what could be another frame for it?" This would shift her frame, and she would be more likely to actually hear what Don was trying to communicate.

Similarly, even though Mike was pleased with his feedback, he might have stepped back and asked himself, "Is there any other way to interpret Don's comments? Was there anything he actually wanted me to change?"

How can you train yourself to be able to step outside of your frame and see things differently? One way is called the ACES Decision-Making Technique.

Aces for the Win

Developed by Dr. Larry Pate in the 1980s, the ACES Decision-Making Technique is a four-phase technique that challenges the frame through which a person is currently viewing a problem and allows them to see it differently.

ACES is an acronym that stands for Assumptions, Criteria, Evoked Set, and Search. *Assumptions* are just what they seem—the assumptions the person is currently making about the problem. ("Don is just being a jerk.") *Criteria* can be described as "What do I want?" ("I want Don to think highly of my work.") *Evoked Set* is an academic term that deals with the question "What are the solutions to the problem you're considering?" ("Maybe I should rewrite the whole report?") *Search* refers to the information the person needs to find in order to solve the problem. ("I guess I better find the sales figures from last month.")

The way the ACES Decision-Making Technique is performed is to take several sheets of paper and write down the current frame on the left hand of the paper (one's current Assumptions, Criteria, and Evoked Set) and then perform a process that allows the person to reverse the Assumptions and Criteria, and add to the Evoked Set. While a complete explanation of the process is beyond the scope of this chapter, the end result is that the person has a list of items on the Search page that will allow them to get more information. The process requires a person to ask, "Under what conditions would the opposite of my assumption be true?"

So when Mary is assuming that Don is being a critical jerk, the opposite of that assumption is that Don is NOT being a critical jerk. She would then ask herself, "Under what conditions would Don NOT be being a critical jerk?" This question allows Mary to step back and think more clearly. "Well, maybe he didn't say it very nicely . . . maybe he was trying to help me make the report better." This isn't to say that in every case the assumption is wrong—maybe Don really IS a critical jerk. But asking the question, "Under what conditions is the opposite true?" allows the listener to reframe the situation.

In the case of Mike and Mary, reframing the situation might have prompted them each to go back to Don and ask, "Do you actually need me to make those revisions, or were they suggestions for improvement for next time?"

When a person actively identifies his or her frame, and then looks at the assumptions he or she is making about the other person, it becomes possible for the listener to hear the speaker's intent the way he or she meant it.

Here is a graphic illustration of how the sender and receiver's filters and frames need to be aligned in order for effective communication to take place.

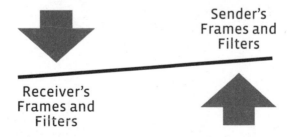

In this chapter, we've talked about some of the factors that affect the Sender's effectiveness in communicating a message. Chapter five continues by looking at other factors, such as the message itself and the environment in which the communication takes place.

> *It takes a great man to be a good listener.*
> —CALVIN COOLIDGE

5. ENCODING FACTORS

*The single biggest problem in communication is
the illusion that it has taken place.*
—GEORGE BERNARD SHAW

It's 4:00 a.m. and the phone rings. "Who could be calling at this hour?" Janet mumbles to herself as she rolls over and grabs the phone. "Hello?"

"Mrs. Vasquez? This is Sergeant Hollister from the police department. I'm afraid I have some bad news . . ."

Janet sits straight up in bed. "What's happened?"

"I'm afraid it's your daughter. There's been an accident. We got a call about 2:30 a.m. about a car on the side of the road . . ."

Janet's mind begins to rush ahead. *Is she OK? Has she been killed?*

"When our patrol officer got to the scene, he was able to identify the license plate . . ."

Come ON. Tell me what happened to my daughter. Is she all right? I can't believe this is happening. I knew we should never have gotten her that car. Oh, my God. My baby. NO! NO!!

"Fortunately, Mrs. Vasquez, your daughter was unhurt. I'm afraid there was alcohol involved and she's been arrested."

Overwhelmed with emotion, Janet can barely understand what she is hearing at this point. *Alcohol? Arrested? What? Thank God she's alive.* Janet breathes a sigh of relief, and with tears in her eyes says, "Thank you so much, officer. I'll be right down to the station."

Encoding the Message

This story illustrates some of the challenges we face when listening to messages. Every time we hear, read, or otherwise receive a message, that message has been encoded in some way.

Encoding means translating the information into a message in the form of symbols that represent ideas or concepts. The symbols can take on numerous forms, such as words, or gestures.

When encoding a message, the sender decides what information he or she wants to transmit. In our story above, Sergeant Hollister has to decide what information he wants to communicate to Janet. He wants to let her know that her daughter has been arrested for drunk driving.

Again, as we remember from a previous chapter, this is influenced by the sender's frames and filters. Sergeant Hollister is a police officer. His natural communication style is very detailed, and he tends to give a lot of information. This stems from his need to fill out police reports.

Because he's coming at the conversation with this frame, he is filtering the information and focusing on *all* of the events, not just the critical thing Janet wants to know: has her daughter been killed?

When encoding messages, it's important for the sender to use symbols that are familiar to the intended receiver. In this case, both Sergeant Hollister and Janet are using verbal communication (as opposed to sign language or writing), and speak the same language, so they are likely to be able to understand each other. Things would be very different if Sergeant Hollister and Janet spoke different languages.

In this scenario, Sergeant Hollister was encoding the message with extraneous information that interfered with Janet's ability to listen. A good way for a sender to encode their message is to mentally visualize the communication from the receiver's point of view. In other words, Sergeant Hollister should have imagined what it would have been like for *him* to get a call at 4:00 in the morning with a difficult message about his teenage daughter. If he'd done so, he might have encoded the message differently.

"Mrs. Vasquez? This is Sergeant Hollister from the police department. I'm afraid I have some bad news . . ."

Janet sits straight up in bed. "What's happened?"

"I'm afraid it's your daughter. *She's not hurt, but* there's been an accident. We got a call about 2:30 a.m. about a car on the side of the road. . ."

By encoding the message so that Janet would have the information that *she* needed to hear—that her daughter was OK—she would have better been able to actually hear what Sergeant Hollister was trying to tell her.

Your success in encoding depends partly on your ability to convey information clearly and simply, partly on your ability to anticipate and eliminate sources of confusion (for example, cultural issues, mistaken assumptions, and missing information). A key part of this process is knowing your audience.

Failure to understand whom you are communicating with will result in delivering messages that are misunderstood.

Relationships Matter

One key factor that influences how we encode messages is the relationship we have with the listener. You're naturally going to encode a message differently for your boss than you do for your best friend or your daughter.

Here are some examples of how a message gets encoded differently, depending on who will be hearing it.

Carrie Quits

Carrie is really unhappy at work and is considering quitting her job. Here is how she'll say that message to different people in her life, using different words that reflect the different concerns the listener might have.

Carrie's best friend: "Oh my god, Pam, I am so sick of my job. My boss is constantly undermining me, my coworkers are annoying, and they do *not* pay me enough money to deal with those rude customers on the phone. I feel like just walking in there and telling my boss I am quitting."

Carrie's husband: "I had another terrible day at work. Mike threw me under the bus in a meeting, Diane was on her personal phone all day, and I had this call from a rude client that had me almost in tears. I'm really not happy with this job. I'm thinking of looking for another one. What do you think?"

Carrie's daughter: "Hi, sweetheart. Mommy wants to talk to you about something. You remember last year when you were in Mrs. Hoyt's class and she was being mean to you, and the other kids were teasing you so badly? Remember how we took you out and got you into another classroom, and how much better things were for you there? Well, the same thing happens sometimes with grownups. I'm sure you hear me telling Daddy about my job. Well, I'm thinking of looking for a different job, where I would be happier. But don't worry. It won't affect you, other than maybe having a happier mommy."

Carrie's boss: "Hi, Mike. Thanks for taking the time to see me. I wanted to talk to you about some concerns I'm having at work here. I'm feeling like my work isn't getting the recognition I feel it should. And when some of my colleagues are taking personal calls during the day, it's a bit distracting. Also, is there a way we can minimize my contact with disgruntled clients? It seems like the customer service reps would be better equipped to handle them. I know we talked about this a few weeks ago, but things really aren't improving, and, actually, I'm considering leaving."

Carrie's relationships with each of the people in this scenario determines how she will encode the message. With her best friend, Carrie is more casual and expresses emotion more freely. With her husband, she gives specific examples and facts to back up her assertions. She also takes more of a collaborative tone. With her daughter, Carrie uses terminology that allows the daughter to relate to what she is saying personally. And with her boss, Carrie takes a problem solving approach.

It's the same message. It's just being encoded with different words, tonality, and emotions.

Dissonant Dyads

Not all relationships are the same, and that's where individual differences come in. For example, some mother-daughter relationships are more "peerlike" ("Do you see that hot guy over there?"), whereas others are more traditional ("Are you seeing anyone new, dear?"). It can be a challenge when one part of the dyad has different expectations than the other. (*Dyad* means "something that consists of two parts.") Here are some examples.

One friend wants to be Best Friends Forever and share every detail of their lives, whereas the other prefers more privacy.

A mother wants to be "friends" with her daughter, but the daughter doesn't want to hear the personal details of her mother's life.

A boss wants to be "casual" with his employee, but the employee doesn't want the boss in his personal life.

Two co-workers working on a project have different ideas about how they will collaborate. One wants to work on every part together, whereas the other wants to divide up the tasks and work independently.

Here are some factors that affect how a message gets encoded.

Encoding Factors

Power Differences	Cultural Differences	Interpersonal Differences
• Parent/Child • Boss/Subordinate • Authority Figure/ Follower	• Race • Nationality • Language	• Gender • Age • Communication Style

The Environment

In addition to the "people" factors that affect the way we encode messages, there are also environmental ones. These include the obvious, like a loud or distracting room. But they also include more subtle things, like the "mood" of the environment.

Have you ever walked into a room, planning on saying something to someone, and as soon as you walked in you changed your mind? Why is this? Perhaps there were clues in the environment that caused you to realize that your message wasn't going to be heard the way you intended. The other person might have been angry, distracted, even sleeping.

Environmental Load

Environmental load is a term that refers to the stress load a person is under. It simply refers to anything in a person's immediate environment that creates a sense of pressure. We've all noticed how communication changes under pressure, when a person is tired, hungry, sick, or otherwise irritable. Examples of load factors are: time pressure, uncertainty, complexity, and the prospect of important consequences, both good and bad.

As a person's environmental load goes up, it affects how much information they need and want to share. Some people under high environmental load get extremely decisive and only want the bare basics of information. Other people tend to "freeze" when they get stressed out and want to look at every available option. You can imagine what happens in communication when the sender and receiver have different styles. We'll get more into how individual differences in environmental load affects communication in the next chapter.

Be Angry at the Message, Not the Messenger

We started this chapter with a scenario where a police officer had to deliver a difficult message to a mother. That is by no means the only situation in which people have to deliver a difficult message. And the difficulty of the message can affect how the sender encodes the message.

Much of the research on delivering bad news comes from medicine. In fact, the American Medical Association first included it in its code of conduct as far back as 1847.

Research published in *The Journal of Trauma Injury Infection and Critical Care* outlines the qualities which family members value most in doctors or nurses who have to communicate bad news. This research shows that, from the receiver's perspective, the four most important factors are (in order of importance):

1. The newsgiver's attitude.
2. The clarity of the message.
3. Privacy.
4. The person's ability to answer questions.

This does a great job of summing up what we have covered in part two of this book so far. The *newsgiver's attitude* is determined by the frame and filter he or she uses. The *clarity* of the message has to do with the encoding factors we're talking about. *Privacy* relates to environmental factors. And *the person's ability to answer questions* has to do with the communication style differences we'll cover in the next chapter.

> *Bad news isn't wine. It doesn't improve with age.*
> —Colin Powell

6. COMMUNICATION STYLE DIFFERENCES

The two words information *and* communication *are often used interchangeably, but they signify quite different things. Information is giving out; communication is getting through.*
—Sydney Harris

A naval submarine officer was training a group of subordinates on the use of some particularly tricky equipment. At one point, he looked up at his students and remarked, "It's hot in here."

Several of the students replied back, "Yes, sir, it is." They then resumed what they were doing.

The officer simply stood there and repeated himself. "It's hot in here."

The students were a bit confused. Again they nodded their heads in agreement, yet did nothing.

Finally the officer explained. "When I tell you 'It's hot in here,' I am not asking for your opinion or agreement. I am conveying that I expect you to do something about it. It's hot in here."

All at once the class scrambled to cool the room down.

They turned on fans and opened vents and then returned to their tasks.*

In this example, the officer might have thought that his subordinates were not listening. He might have gotten angry or just gone to solve the problem himself. But because this was a military environment, he was teaching his subordinates that when a commanding officer gives you a piece of information, it's to be acted upon.

This chapter will focus on the elements that lead to differences in communication style between people. These differences are important, because if the sender and receiver don't understand each other, it can be a barrier to communication. The subordinates in our example above didn't understand why the officer was commenting on the temperature, so they didn't hear that he wanted them to take action.

Decision Styles

At the basis of most communication, as we've mentioned before, is a decision about how, what, and when to share information. Looking at individual differences in decision style can help us understand how senders and receivers perceive the information that is being communicated.

One particular framework for identifying decision styles is based upon a conceptual model originally devel-

---

* Story adapted from Deborah Tannen, *Talking from 9 to 5: Women and Men at Work* (New York: William Morrow, 1990), 87.

oped by Michael J. Driver and then further defined by Driver and Kenneth Brousseau. It's called the Driver Decision Style Model and explores how people make decisions on two dimensions—the amount of information they use when making decisions, and how many alternatives the person considers when making a decision.

Information Use

People differ widely in the amount of information they use in decisionmaking. Some people reach conclusions on the basis of just a few facts. Others reach conclusions only after gathering and studying large amounts of information. Those who use low amounts of information are called *Satisficers*. The term *satisficing* means to use a few pieces of information to come up with a decision that is "good enough."

The opposites of Satisficers are *Maximizers*. These are the people who take a lot of information into account before making a decision.

According to Driver and Brousseau, "Satisficers know that there is more information that they could take into consideration, and their tendency is to want to get on with things. They prefer to keep moving, rather than 'analyzing things to death.' At the other extreme is the maximizer mode. Maximizers want to be sure that they have considered all of the relevant facts, and that they have missed no important details, no matter how subtle. Their interest is in coming up with a high quality solution or in learning something new and important."

Now let's imagine a conversation between a Maximizer and a Satisficer. It's a married couple, planning a vacation.

> Cheryl: Honey, will you sit down with me and help me plan our summer vacation? I'm not sure if we should take a cruise or go to an all-inclusive resort. And even then, where do we go? We could go to Hawaii again. Or maybe Europe this time. Let's take a look at a few travel review websites and get some information. Oh, and I'll put a post on Facebook to see where my friends went on vacation.
> Ed: A cruise is fine. Or a resort. I don't really want to go to Hawaii again. Let's do Europe. You find out a couple of destinations and we can talk then.

Cheryl is clearly a Maximizer. She wants to consider as much information as possible when making a decision. Ed, on the other hand, is a Satisficer. He's not concerned with making the best choice. He feels that whatever he does, as long as he's not at work and with his family, he'll be happy.

Imagine how this conversation could have gone wrong. Cheryl could have been mad that Ed didn't want to listen to all of the different options and alternatives. She might have taken it to mean that he's not excited about the trip or that he doesn't care about her.

Ed might have thought that Cheryl was being overly analytical and wasting time getting too much information. He could easily have stopped listening to her as she was going through all the different options because, from his point of view, he didn't need to hear every possibility.

As a result, he's not listening. She's mad, and he's confused. This is why understanding decision styles is so important in communication!

Focus

As mentioned, the Driver Decision Styles Model also uses *focus* as one of the dimensions of how people make decisions. People tend to fall on one or the other end of a spectrum when it comes to focus. There are "uni-focus" people, who are focused on generating one best solution, and there are "multi-focus" people, who tend to see different solutions or options as equally appealing.

Driver and Brousseau say,

Uni-focus decision-makers tend to have very strong views about how things ought to be done. Faced with any situation, they usually have a very specific criterion in mind, such as cost, quality, or fairness, by which they will evaluate any potential solution. So, they usually will find a solution that stacks up best according to their criterion or goal.

Multi-focus thinkers, on the other hand, often use many criteria to evaluate potential solutions. They tend to have many goals. So, whereas one solution may fit some criteria very well, another course of action may fit other criteria better. Consequently, they are more open to alternatives and are more conditional in their thinking. This conditional way of thinking rubs uni-focus decision-makers the wrong way. To them, it appears as though their multi-focus associates are confused, wishy-washy, lacking in values, or simply "flakey." On the other hand, the strong, highly focused views of the uni-focus people strike the multi-focus thinkers as being rigid, narrow, unyielding, and dogmatic. When the tension escalates, these rather polite descriptors give way to even more colorful adjectives!

Four Primary Styles

As a result, using both dimensions, we have four possible combinations.

Maximizer Uni-Focus. People who make careful and slow decisions based on a lot of information and analysis. They want to find the best solution to the matter at hand. They are called *Hierarchic*.

Maximizer Multi-Focus. These people are ones who use a lot of information and are happy to consider a lot of options. To them, decisionmaking is a process, not a singular event. They are called *Integrative*.

Satisficer Uni-Focus. People who use a minimum amount of information to quickly come to a clear decision about a course of action. They are called *Decisive*.

Satisficer Multi-Focus. These people have very fluid thinking styles. Any piece of information will be seen as having different interpretations and implications. If the course of action they choose isn't working, they'll quickly move to another. They are called *Flexible*.

Here are some phrases. See if you can tell which style would say it.

A: "Life is too short to waste time. Just say what you have to say and be done with it. Don't give me all the background, just tell me what I need to know."

B: "There's no point in arguing about it. It's all good. If it doesn't work out, we'll just change it. Just relax."

C: "There's no need to rush to judgment here. If something is worth doing, it's worth doing right. Let's take our time and make sure we make the best decision."

D: "I have an opinion, but I'd like to hear what everyone else has to say. Let's see if we can't come up with an innovative and creative solution."

Can you tell which style said each phrase? The answers are at the bottom of the page.*

Think about the people in your life. Who do you know that is each of the different styles? Which style are you?

Role Style Versus Operating Style

There is one other factor in the model that affects what style a person demonstrates when making decisions and communicating.

People tend to behave differently when they are in public than they do in their private lives. Going back to the

---

* A: Decisive; B: Flexible; C: Hierarchic; D: Integrative.

example in a previous chapter, with Carrie wanting to quit her job, she's likely to use a different style with her boss than with her best friend. Those differences are called *Role Style* and *Operating Style*.

When people are aware that they need to present a favorable image, such as in a job interview, giving a speech, or meeting potential in-laws for the first time, they tend to behave in a manner that is appropriate for the role. The person behaves the way they think they should behave, not necessarily in their natural style.

When a person is less aware of how he or she is thinking or behaving, the natural style comes out. This is the "real" person, not the one shown in public.

It's Different With Friends

There's a classic scene in the movie *Grease* where Danny Zuko runs into his summer romance, Sandy Olson, thanks to their mutual friend Rizzo.

Rizzo: Hey Zuko! I've got a surprise for you.

Danny: Oh, yeah?

Rizzo: [chuckles] Yeah.

Danny: [throws Sandy in front of him] Sandy!

Sandy: Danny!

Danny: Wha-what are you doing here? I thought you were moving back to Australia?

Sandy: We were, but we had a change in plans!

His friends stare at Danny with a strange face and he changes moods, pretending he doesn't care.

Danny then switches from his Operating Style—the "real" Danny, who is happy to see Sandy—to his Role Style—the Danny who feels he "should" act tough in front of his friends.

Danny: That's cool baby, you know how it is, rockin' and rollin' and whatnot.

Sandy: Danny?

Danny: That's my name, don't wear it out.

Sandy: What's the matter with you?

Danny: What's the matter with me, baby, what's the matter with you?

Sandy: What happened to the Danny Zuko I met at the beach?

Danny: Well I do not know. Maybe there's two of us. Why don't you take out a missing person's ad? Or try the yellow pages, I don't know.

Sandy: You're a fake and a phony and I wish I never laid eyes on you!

You can see from this interaction how understanding Operating and Role styles can prevent a lot of conflict. If Sandy were able to see that Danny had to put up a "tough guy" image with his friends, she wouldn't have taken it personally. If Danny understood the difference between Role

Style and Operating Style, he might have found a way to convey to Sandy that he was really happy to see her. In fact, the rest of the movie plays off the dynamic between the Role and Operating styles of communication.

This chapter has gone into some of the communication style differences between people that affect how we decide how, what, and when to share information. A mismatch between people can cause serious miscommunications, leading to conflict. Part three investigates the different kinds of communication breakdowns and explores ways to reduce them.

> *Think like a wise man but communicate in the*
> *language of the people.*
> —WILLIAM BUTLER YEATS

My Listening Log, Part Two

Sender Frames

On another piece of paper or in a journal, answer the following questions.

1. Describe an experience you had where someone was communicating to you with a frame that biased their view. Were you able to see it clearly at the time?

2. Who in your life tends to communicate using the same frame as you most often? How are your frames similar?

3. Whom do you have the most difficulty communicating with in your life?

4. Describe an instance in which someone said something that made you angry.

5. What is the reason you believe they acted that way?

6. Now challenge that reason. If you said, "Because he was being selfish," then reverse it. "He was NOT being selfish." Write the reverse assumption down.

7. Ask yourself, "Under what conditions could the reverse assumption be true?"

Encoding the Message

When encoding a message, the sender decides what information he or she wants to transmit.

---

1. You need to convey the following message to certain people: "I am moving to another state next month." How would you encode the message differently for each person?
   a. Your parents or extended family
   b. Your boss
   c. Your best friend
   d. Your children
   e. Facebook and other social media

2. Describe a time when the following factors influenced how someone encoded a message to you.
   a. Power differences
   b. Cultural differences
   c. Interpersonal differences

Environmental Factors in Encoding

Environmental load is a term that refers to the stress load a person is under.

---

1. Recall a time when you walked into a room and could instantly sense a "vibe" or mood in the room. What was going on?

2. Encode the following messages based on different environmental loads.
   a. Tell someone to turn left on an empty street.
   b. Tell someone to turn left in heavy traffic from the right lane.
   c. Respond to someone interrupting what you're doing at work, under a deadline.
   d. Respond to someone interrupting what you're doing at work at 4:45 on a Friday.

Decision Styles

"Satisficing" means to use a few pieces of information to come up with a decision that is "good enough."

Maximizers are the people who consider a LOT of information before making a decision.

On another piece of paper or a journal, answer the following questions.

1. Whom do you know who is a Satisficer?

2. Who is a Maximizer?

3. Which are you?

4. Give an example of a time when you demonstrated each type of information use.

"Uni-focus" people are focused on generating one best solution. "Multi-focus" people tend to see different solutions or options as equally appealing.

---

5. Do you tend to be a uni-focus person or a multi-focus person?

6. Describe a time when you had a conflict with a person who has the other style of focus. Would knowing this information have helped deescalate the conflict? How?

Four Styles

Hierarchic: People who make careful and slow decisions based on a lot of information and analysis.

Integrative: People who use a lot of information and are happy to consider a lot of options.

Decisive: People who use a minimum amount of information to quickly come to a clear decision about a course of action.

Flexible: People who have very fluid thinking styles, using a small amount of information in a lot of different ways.

1. Describe a typical career choice for each of the four styles. (Sample answers are at the bottom of this page, although these aren't the only correct ones.)*

Hierarchic
Integrative
Decisive
Flexible

_____

Role Style: Behaving the way you think you should behave in a given situation.

Operating Style: Your natural decision style

_____

* a. accountant, engineer; b. writer, scientist; c. surgeon, fighter pilot; d. therapist, teacher

2. Describe whether you would be in Role Style or Operating Style in the following situations.
    a. A parent/teacher conference.
    b. Watching a movie on the couch with your best friend.
    c. In a computer training class at work.
    d. After the computer training class, at happy hour with your co-workers.

PART THREE

You're Not Listening!

*Communication
Breakdowns*

7. CONFLICT

No one would talk much in society if he
knew how often he misunderstands others.
—Johann Wolfgang von Goethe

Elizabeth is excited. She's been dating her boyfriend, Andy, for a year and a half now, and they are finally going away for a long holiday weekend alone. Andy has three kids from his marriage and shares custody of them with his ex-wife, Michelle. Between their busy work schedules and the kids being at Andy's house every other weekend, Elizabeth and Andy haven't had much time for just the two of them.

It's Thursday evening, and Elizabeth is standing in front of her closet, deciding which outfits to bring, when her phone rings. She sees that it's Andy.

"Hi sweetheart," Elizabeth says. "I am SO excited about our weekend. I'm just starting to pack."

"Hey. Yeah, that's why I'm calling."

Elizabeth's heart sinks, and her stomach starts to tighten. She can hear something in Andy's voice. "What's up?" she asks suspiciously.

"Well, you know that this weekend is supposed to be my weekend with the kids, right?"

"Yes . . ."

"Well, turns out that the ski trip that they were going to go on with their cousins has been canceled. I guess the mom came down with the flu or something. So . . . I've got the kids this weekend."

"Can't you call Michelle and see if she can take them? She IS their mother after all." Elizabeth can feel herself getting really upset. This was supposed to be THEIR weekend!

"I don't really think I can do that. You know I just had to take her to court to get more custody of the kids. I can't very well turn around and ask her to take them."

Elizabeth can feel the tears stinging her eyes. She knows that she should be gracious and accepting, yet she feels so disappointed that she can't hold back the sarcasm in her voice. "No, of course not. You wouldn't dare ask your EX-WIFE to watch her own children. Instead, you'd ask ME to once again put our relationship aside so that the kids can sit at your house and play video games all weekend."

"What if we all went away somewhere together? We could go skiing. I know it's not the same, but we could still have some time alone together while the kids . . ."

Elizabeth interrupts. "No. Forget it. I am not sitting in some cramped cabin with three kids and calling it a romantic weekend. You guys just go without me."

Now it's Andy's turn to get mad. "Look. You knew I had kids when we started dating. I made it clear then that my kids come first. I'm sorry. None of this is my fault. If that's how you want to be, then fine. I WILL take the kids skiing. You are welcome to come with us, or not. I'd rather have you be with us. But it's your call."

"I just don't understand why you always put Michelle before me. I'm supposed to be your girlfriend . . . I guess you just don't want anyone knowing that our relationship is important. Or maybe what's really going on is that our relationship ISN'T important to you. I need some time to think about if this is the relationship for me. I've got to go."

Elizabeth hangs up, and each of them stands there staring at their phones, upset at how quickly the conversation escalated into a relationship-threatening argument.

Conflict is present is just about every kind of relationship. From intimate ones, to professional ones, communication breakdowns wreak havoc on relationships. This chapter will examine how conflict develops and how effective listening skills can prevent and resolve interpersonal conflict in relationships.

Mixed Messages

Regardless of the content of the conversation, the sender, the receiver, or the environment, interpersonal conflict results from a breakdown in communication between two people. It's exacerbated when there are strong emotions on both sides.

*Interpersonal conflict results
from a breakdown in communication
between two people.*

In the scenario above, Andy has to deliver some news to Elizabeth. Here's an illustration of that communication at its basics.

We can see that in and of itself, the message doesn't create conflict. It's a statement of fact. Andy has his kids this weekend.

The conflict comes from the different frames each person has about the message. Andy's frame is that because he has his kids unexpectedly for the weekend, he and Elizabeth can find an alternate plan that allows them all to get away for the holiday. Elizabeth's frame is that Andy's kids coming for the weekend changes the experience she planned on having.

Here is a visual representation of this situation.

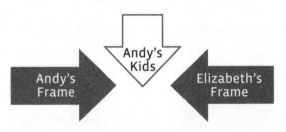

When you look at it visually like this, it's easy to see how the situation can trigger strong emotions on either side. Like most parents, Andy feels strong loyalty to his kids. If he feels that someone is trying to come between him and his kids, he'll become defensive and emotional.

Elizabeth, on the other hand, wants to feel important to Andy. She knows he loves his kids, yet she sees the kids coming between him and her.

Stages Of Conflict

Conflict develops in stages, and they are usually pretty predictable. Managing conflict involves identifying how and when conflict happens in the first place.

In 1967, researcher Lou Pondy presented a model of organizational conflict that identified five stages of conflict.

1. **Latent conflict**: the potential for conflict.
2. **Perceived conflict**: this is the cognitive aspect where one or both parties may recognize that there is a conflict.
3. **Felt conflict**: this is the "feeling" aspect of conflict—parties begin to feel upset.
4. **Manifest conflict**: this is the behavioral aspect of conflict. Hostility, arguing, or physical altercation.
5. **Conflict aftermath**: the effects of conflict.

Here's how these stages apply to our scenario above.

Latent conflict: When Andy calls Elizabeth to tell her that he will have his kids for the weekend, interrupting their plans, there is the potential for conflict.

Perceived conflict: Immediately upon hearing Andy's tone, Elizabeth begins to become aware that there is a conflict.

Felt conflict: Upon hearing Andy's message, Elizabeth begins to feel upset.

Manifest conflict: They begin arguing. Note that manifest conflict can cycle backwards: Andy begins to be aware that Elizabeth is angry. He then gets angry at her manifest conflict, and begins to manifest conflict himself by suggesting that he will take the kids away for the weekend without her.

Conflict aftermath: The effect of the conflict is that both Andy and Elizabeth reevaluate the entire relationship and consider breaking up.

Leftover Latent Conflict

This particular weekend conflict didn't arise in isolation. Andy and Elizabeth have been together for a year and a half. The more experiences each person has from previous communication problems (both in this relationship and in others), the more likely latent conflict is to turn into manifest conflict.

*The more experiences each person
has from previous communication problems,
the more likely latent conflict is to
turn into manifest conflict.*

For example, Andy and his ex-wife Michelle have been arguing about the kids since they were married. He just ended a bitter court battle. So he's bringing that into the conversation with Elizabeth.

Meanwhile, Elizabeth has been through a year and a half where her boyfriend was distracted and upset over a court battle with his ex-wife over the children. This weekend is not the first time that Elizabeth's needs have been put aside because of Michelle.

Three Phases of Conflict Resolution

In his book *The Power of Ethical Persuasion*, Dr. Tom Rusk offers a three-phase model of conflict resolution. The three phases are:

Phase One: Explore the other person's viewpoint.
Phase Two: Explain your viewpoint.
Phase Three: Create resolutions.

Here's a little more about each of the three phases.

Phase One: Explore the Other Person's Viewpoint

You'll note that this comes BEFORE the phase where you explain your own viewpoint. This is the mistake that so many people make in conflictual situations. We spend so much time trying to get the other person to hear our side and fail to explore their viewpoint.

This, again, relates to frames and learning how to shift them. You've got to be able to step outside your own frame and explore the other person's frame.

Dr. Rusk gives seven steps to exploring the other person's viewpoint.

1. Establish that your immediate goal is mutual understanding, not problem solving.

2. Elicit the other person's thoughts, feelings, and desires about the subject at hand.

3. Ask for the other person's help in understanding him or her. Try not to defend or disagree.

4. Repeat the other person's position in your own words to show you understand.

5. Ask the other person to correct your understanding and keep restating his or her position.

6. Refer back to your position only to keep things going.

7. Repeat steps 1 through 6 until the other person unreservedly agrees that you understand his or her position.

> *We spend so much time trying to get the other person to hear our side that we fail to explore the other person's viewpoint.*

Phase Two: Explain Your Viewpoint

Only after you have fully listened to the other person's viewpoint and established their frame can you then focus on explaining your own viewpoint. If you try to share yours prematurely, the other person won't feel "heard" and won't be able to hear you in return.

Here are five steps for explaining your viewpoint.

1. Ask for a fair hearing in return.

2. Begin with an explanation of how the other person's thoughts and feelings affect you.

3. Avoid blaming and self-defense as much as possible.

4. Carefully explain your thoughts, desires, and feelings as *your* truth, not *the* truth.

5. Ask for restatements of your position—and corrections of any factual inaccuracies—as necessary.

6. Review your respective positions.

Only after you have fully listened to the other person's viewpoint and established their frame can you then focus on explaining your own viewpoint.

Phase Three: Create Resolutions

Once each of you has listened to the other person fully, you're then ready to explore options to create a resolution.

One way to look at it is to envision both of you on opposite sides of a table. In the middle of the table is a piece of paper that represents the issue or problem.

In typical conflict situations, each side is focused on getting the piece of paper over to their side of the table. "We're going to go away for the weekend alone." "We're going to bring the kids with us."

In this model, by contrast, both of the parties will come over to the same side of the table and look at the piece of paper together, solving the problem in a collaborative manner, instead of battling over who gets to have the paper on their side of the table.

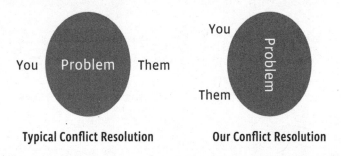

Typical Conflict Resolution   **Our Conflict Resolution**

When both of you are on the same side and are focusing on the problem to be solved, conflict decreases. And, of course, it all starts with listening.

Here are some tips for creating resolutions.

1. Affirm your mutual understanding and confirm that you are both ready to consider options for resolution.

2. Brainstorm multiple options.

3. If a mutually agreeable solution is not yet obvious, try one or more of the following options:

   • Take time out to reconsider, consult, exchange proposals, and reconvene.

   • Agree to neutral arbitration, mediation, or counseling.

   • Compromise between alternate solutions.

   • Take turns between alternate solutions.

   • Yield (for now) once your position is thoroughly and respectfully considered.

   • Assert your positional power after thoroughly and respectfully considering their position.

   • Agree to disagree and still respect each other; then, if you can, go your separate ways on this issue.

Andy and Elizabeth Revisited

Let's revisit the scenario with Andy and Elizabeth, applying what we've learned in this chapter.

Here's the conversation again, up to the point where the conflict went from being latent to being perceived.

It's Thursday evening and Elizabeth is standing in front of her closet, deciding which outfits to bring, when her phone rings. She sees that it's Andy.

"Hi, sweetheart," Elizabeth says. "I am SO excited about our weekend. I'm just starting to pack."

"Hey. Yeah, that's why I'm calling."

Elizabeth's heart sinks, and her stomach starts to tighten. She can hear something in Andy's voice. "What's up?" she asks suspiciously.

"Well, you know that this weekend is supposed to be my weekend with the kids, right?"

"Yes . . ."

"Well, turns out that the ski trip that they were going to go on with their cousins has been canceled. I guess the mom came down with the flu or something. So . . . I've got the kids this weekend."

"Can't you call Michelle and see if she can take them? She IS their mother after all." Elizabeth can feel herself getting really upset. This was supposed to be THEIR weekend!

At this point, both Andy and Elizabeth are cognitively aware that there is a conflict, and are beginning to feel it emotionally. Remember the three phases of conflict resolution:

Phase One: Explore the other person's viewpoint.
Phase Two: Explain your viewpoint.
Phase Three: Create resolutions.

Here's how the conversation could have gone differently.

"Hey, Elizabeth. I'm on your side here. I can hear you're upset. Tell me what you're feeling."

"I'm feeling frustrated, that's what. It seems like every time we plan to do something together. Michelle gets in the way. It's not the kids that are the problem. I feel that Michelle is jealous of our relationship."

Note that Andy has a decision point here. He could disagree with Elizabeth, thus escalating the argument. Or he can continue to ask questions to elicit her feelings.

"I can certainly see why you feel that way. You and I have gotten very close over the past year and a half. So, if I understand correctly, it's not only about this weekend. It's about a pattern of our plans getting interrupted, is that right?"

"Yes, that's exactly right."

Only now that he has Elizabeth's agreement that she has been "heard" can Andy then go and explain his position.

"OK, so now that I understand your feelings, will you give me a fair hearing in return?"

"Sure. OK."

"When you get disappointed like that, it makes me feel like I am the one disappointing you. And I never EVER want to do that. I love you!"

"I love you, too."

"And the thing is, this was totally outside of my control. Maybe you're right and Michelle is jealous of us. Ever since the divorce she has been bad-mouthing me to the kids. I don't want to give her anything else bad to say, like 'Your dad didn't even want to be with you on his weekend. He only asked for more time with you to save money on child support.' So that's why I don't want to ask her to take the kids. I don't want to disappoint them either."

"Yeah, I can see that."

"So I'm trying to find a solution that doesn't disappoint anyone."

"I know. I can't help but be disappointed. I was so looking forward to alone time with you. But they are just kids and I'm a grownup. I can handle my disappointment."

Now Andy and Elizabeth are ready to work on solving the problem.

"So what do we do?"

"How about taking the kids skiing this weekend, and then we going to the bed and breakfast next weekend? I know you'll have to work a bit in the mornings, but we'd have the rest of the day to play."

You can see that there are different ways the conversation could have played out. Elizabeth might have taken the lead on exploring Andy's feelings first, for example. Or they could have come up with different solutions. The key, though, is that they each took the time to LISTEN to the other person's point of view and explore the other person's frame.

This chapter has touched on the tricky area of conflict in interpersonal relationships. We've established that listening skills are critical to avoiding and deescalating conflict.

The next chapter will help you explore your own conflict style so that you can become a better listener when latent conflict becomes perceived.

> *Relationships are based on feelings . . .*
> *Upset feelings give you an opportunity to*
> *deepen a relationship . . . The key . . . is to*
> *handle them all with caring and respect.*
> —DR. TOM RUSK

8. YOUR CONFLICT STYLE
(and What It Says about Listening)

One of our strongest weapons is dialogue.
—NELSON MANDELA

As Bill walks down the hall toward the conference room, he can feel a headache coming on. *This is the worst part about being the boss*, he thinks. But being the boss means you have to be the one to have the tough conversations. And if he doesn't address this issue now, things could escalate.

"Mike, Tom, Lin, Karen, thanks for coming in. I'm sure you all know why I've called this meeting." As the four members of Bill's management team file into the room, he can already sense the tension between them.

"I, for one, am glad we are having this meeting, Bill," Mike says loudly. "I'll be glad to stop all this infighting once everyone hears that you and I are in alignment as to what the problem REALLY is." Mike glares at Tom, who averts his eyes.

Bill continues on. "The four of you are my management team. But in the past three months, the conflict between you all has increased, and I'm now getting complaints from people on your teams. Ever since the merger, each department has been running things in different ways, and it's starting to become a serious problem. We need to come to consensus about the policies and procedures and then apply them uniformly across the organization."

Lin steps in. "I'm sure if we could just work together we can come up with a solution together, that would be better than anything we could come up with individually."

Karen replies, "I just hate all this tension. We all have relationships with each other and that's what we should be focusing on. I, for one, am willing to drop the whole conflict if everyone else is willing to do the same."

The group can see that Mike is getting visibly upset. "No! It's not about our relationships with each other or coming to some kind of group consensus. This is a matter of principle at this point." He looks at Bill. "Tell them! Tell them that I'm right!"

Bill folds his hands as he looks at the team. Tom has been notably silent throughout the whole meeting. "Tom, what do you think?"

Tom takes a moment before speaking. "I don't see what the big deal is. It's really not worth it to be fighting like this. I don't really have an opinion, so I'm just listening to what everyone else has to say."

"Of course you don't have an opinion, Tom!" Mike is practically yelling now. "You never do. You and I are the only managers left from the old organization. Instead of standing up for the way we did things before—which, I might add, led to the success that caused the merger in the first place—you just back down!"

"That's one way of looking at it, Mike," Lin offers. "It seems to me that the way we were doing things before wasn't working all that well. I really do think that we should try to brainstorm solutions."

"Fine . . . I give in." Karen is practically in tears. "We can do it your way. I just want to go back to having a happy workplace."

Conflict, whether in the workplace or in personal life, is traumatic. And, as we've mentioned, it affects (and is affected by) the parties' ability to listen effectively.

The scenario above illustrates how having different ways of handling conflict can actually escalate problems instead of resolving them.

This chapter will cover five basic conflict styles and will discuss how to use effective listening to minimize conflict with each.

It's important to note that there has been a lot of research done on interpersonal conflict styles, and the model we present here is a hybrid of many of those approaches. Conflict management is an entire field of inquiry that is beyond the scope of this book.

Different Conflict Styles

For the purposes of this book, we've identified four basic styles that people fall into when faced with conflict.* They are:

The Lion. This style values "winning the point" more than the relationship. They see conflict as a competition. "I know they'll come around once they see my point." It's an "I win/you lose" position.

The Ostrich. This style avoids conflict at all costs. To them, having conflict IS the problem, and it's not worth the trouble to argue, because it won't affect the outcome anyway. "I'd rather just forget it." This is an "I lose/you lose" position.

The Dog. This style values the relationship above all else and will accommodate to the other person's desires for the sake of maintaining the relationship. It's the exact opposite of the Lion. "Fine, we'll just do it your way." It's an "I lose/you win" approach.

The Fish. Like a school of fish, this style focuses on collaboration and working together. They want to explore the different options in order to come up with one where everyone benefits. It's an "I win/you win" approach.

---

* This model is based on "Conflict Management Questionnaire"; http://academic.engr.arizona.edu/vjohnson/SelfAssessment%20documents/Conflict%20Management%20Questionnaire.doc; accessed Aug. 17, 2016.

There's another style that's not so much a dominant style. Instead it's a state that one can adopt to help someone else move from one style to another. We're calling it *the Chameleon*. This is the person who adopts the other styles momentarily in order to communicate with someone with another style.

As with Role Style versus Operating Style, there are many variables that influence how a person handles conflict. We each have a natural tendency to handle conflict a certain way, although factors such as environmental load, the power relationship with the other person, cultural differences, and similar things can influence whether we'll use our natural style or another style.

It's also important to note that one style is not necessarily better than another. It might seem that the Fish, for example, is the ideal style, since it focuses on creating a win/win. But there are circumstances where collaborating for the win might NOT be the best style (in business competition, for example).

What's Your Conflict Style?

Following is a questionnaire that will help you discover your own conflict style. When answering the questions, remember that there is no right or better answer. Each style is good in its own way.

Score your answer by rating how much you agree with the statement.

6 = definitely true
5 = true
4 = tends to be true
3 = tends to not be true
2 = not true
1 = definitely not true

1. I'm focused on getting excellent results, but other people tend to stand in my way.

2. I am always willing to listen to other's opinions, and I also want to give them mine

3. I often change my goals in order for other people to get theirs.

4. If people don't respect my opinion, I keep it to myself.

5. When someone else has an idea that they think is good, I try to help them.

6. When there's a conflict, I won't vary from my principles, no matter what.

7. I am always willing to consider other people's opinions, but I make my own decisions.

8. In times of conflict, it's more important that a solution be reached than it is to get my priorities met.

9. When a conflict occurs, I tend to back out of the situation and do something else.

10. I don't like causing conflict, so I cooperate with others and do what they want.

11. When pursuing my priorities, I hold firm to what I want.

12. During a conflict, I immediately work to get everyone's concerns out in the open.

13. During a conflict, I try to find some compromise.

14. Differences of opinion are not always worth worrying about, so I usually avoid them.

15. I like to ask others for their opinions and try to find ways to cooperate.

16. Once I have taken a position, I don't like to have others try to talk me out of it.

17. When there is a conflict, I want to hear everyone's point of view, and to express my own.

18. When people have different viewpoints, I generally propose a middle ground.

19. I tend to avoid people who are very opinionated.

20. I think it is more important to get along than to win an argument.

21. After I have made a decision, I'll defend it passionately.

22. I am a decisive person, yet I make a point of listening to others to find the best solution possible.

24. When I see others arguing about something, I keep to myself, because it doesn't do any good to argue.

25. If someone feels more strongly about something than I do, I'll adjust my priorities.

How to Figure Out Your Score

For each of the following categories, write down the number you wrote for the question, and then add them together.

Lion

1: _____

6: _____

11: _____

16: _____

21: _____

Total _____

Fish

2: _____

12: _____

13: _____

17: _____

24: _____

Total _____

Ostrich

4: _____

9: _____

14: _____

19: _____

22: _____

Total _____

Chameleon

5: _____

7: _____

15: _____

20: _____

25: _____

Total _____

Dog

3: _____

8: _____

10: _____

18: _____

23: _____

Total _____

What does this mean?

Results

My dominant style is _____ (Your HIGHEST score)
and my backup style is _____ (Your second highest score)

In our opening scenario, then, here is the conflict style of
the various people.

> Mike: Lion
> Tom: Ostrich
> Karen: Dog
> Lin: Fish
> Bill: Chameleon

When To Use Each Style*

This model reflects the CHOICES that people make in
given situations, not ingrained personality traits. There
are some circumstances in which each style is appropriate.
Here are some examples of when each style is preferred.

Lion
• When conflict involves personal differences that are
  difficult to change.
• When fostering intimate or supportive relationships is
  not critical.
• When others are likely to take advantage of
  noncompetitive behavior.

---

* Adapted from Anthony Falikowski, *Mastering Human Relations*, 3rd ed. (Don
Mills, Ontario: Pearson Education Canada, 2002).

- When conflict resolution is urgent; a crisis when a decision is vital.
- When unpopular decisions need to be implemented.

Ostrich
- When the stakes are not high or the issue is trivial.
- When confrontation will hurt a working relationship.
- When there is little chance of satisfying your wants.
- When disruption outweighs benefit of conflict resolution.
- When gathering information is more important than an immediate decision.
- When others can more effectively resolve the conflict.
- When time constraints demand a delay.

Dog
- When maintaining the relationship outweighs other considerations.
- When the suggestions or changes are not important to the accommodator.
- When minimizing losses in situations where one is outmatched or losing.
- When time is limited.
- When harmony and stability are valued.

Fish
- When maintaining relationships is important.
- When time is not a concern.
- When peer conflict is involved.

- When trying to gain commitment through consensus building.
- When learning and trying to merge differing perspectives.

Chameleon
- When important or complex issues leave no clear or simple solutions.
- When all conflicting people are equal in power and have strong interests in different solutions.
- When there are no time restraints.

Understanding these styles is the first step to improving our ability to listen to each other. If you're in a meeting, for example, and tensions are running high, look around the room and see what style the others are engaging in. Is there a Lion? Who is the Ostrich? By identifying the styles that the other people are expressing, we are better able to step outside our own frame and into the frame of the other person. As we have been saying all along, that's the first step in effective listening.

POX for Peace

Your two best friends, Sam and Noah, are fighting, and once again you're caught in the middle. You really just want them to start agreeing with each other. Is there anything you can do to smooth things over?

In 1946, theorist Fritz Heider developed something called Balance Theory to examine relationships between people and things. It can be best visualized as a triangle, with the points labeled P (person), O (other), and X (a third element).

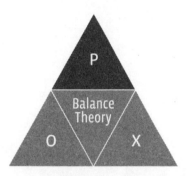

In our example, you are P; Sam is O, the other person; and X is the other element, Noah. When the state is balanced, all three elements have a positive association with each other.

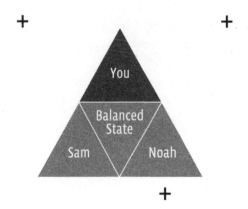

But when one of the positives becomes a negative (Sam and Noah are arguing, for example), the system becomes imbalanced.

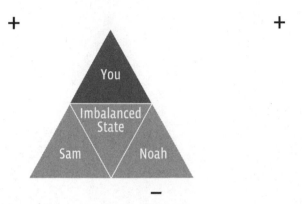

My friend's friend is my friend.
My friend's enemy is my enemy.
My enemy's friend is my enemy.
My enemy's enemy is my friend.

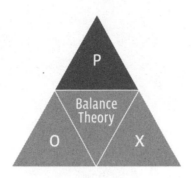

There are four sets of relationships that are usually balanced:

- P + O, P + X, O + X
- P − O, P − X, O + X
- P − O, P + X, O − X
- P+O, P − X, O − X

There are also four typically unbalanced relationships that are likely to be turned into the above balanced relationships:

- P + O, P − X, O + X
- P + O, P + X, O − X
- P − O, P + X, O + X
- P − O, P − X, O − X

Examples
   Balanced: P + O, P + X, O + X: You agree with Sam. You agree with Noah. Sam agrees with Noah.
   Unbalanced: P + O, P + X, O − X: You agree with Sam. You agree with Noah. Sam doesn't agree with Noah.

When the system is unbalanced, something called *dissonance* occurs. Dissonance is the psychological tension that occurs whenever there is an unbalance. Our minds want to restore balance. One way to do this is through understanding the conflict style of the other people in the triad.

Restoring Balance

In order to restore balance and deescalate conflict, you've got to listen carefully to each person, identify their style, and then frame the situation according to their style. Here's how that might look for each of the styles.

The Lion. This style is competitive. They value "winning the point" more than the relationship. Demonstrate how agreement is actually "winning."

The Ostrich. This style avoids conflict at all costs. Show the Ostrich that there really is no conflict. There is just a different way of seeing things.

The Dog. This style values the relationship above all else and will accommodate to the other person's desires for the sake of maintaining the relationship. With the Dog, focus on the relationship between all three of you.

The Fish. Like a school of fish, this style focuses on collaboration and working together. They want to explore the different options to come up with one where everyone benefits. Again, this is a technique more than a style. This is what you are doing when you're trying to reestablish balance.

This chapter has covered the basic styles that people have when facing conflict, and brought forth a model that shows how imbalance happens. In part four, we'll explore some effective listening techniques that will allow you to hear the information you need in order to solve—and prevent—communication breakdowns.

> *Sensitivity to others is no trivial skill; rather,*
> *it is a truly precious human ability. But it isn't*
> *complex: it requires receptiveness to other people*
> *and a willingness to listen.*
> —James Kouzes and Barry Posner

My Listening Log
Part Three

Stages of Conflict

Conflict comes from the different frames each person has about the message.

Let's review the five stages of conflict:

1. **Latent conflict:** the potential for conflict.

2. **Perceived conflict:** this is the cognitive aspect where one or both parties may recognize that there is a conflict.

3. **Felt conflict:** this is the "feeling" aspect of conflict—parties begin to feel upset.

4. **Manifest conflict:** this is the behavioral aspect of conflict. Hostility, arguing, or physical altercation.

5. **Conflict aftermath:** The effects of conflict.

In a notebook or a journal, answer the following questions.

1. Describe a relationship you have that often has latent conflict.

2. When was the last time you cognitively perceived conflict developing in a conversation? Did the other person recognize it too?

3. How do you react to "felt" conflict? What feelings do you have?

4. What is the worst thing you ever did during manifest conflict?

5. What was the aftermath of your answer to question 4?

Three Phases of Conflict Resolution

It might help for you to role-play these exercises with another person to get the most out of the practice. Just be sure not to choose the person you had the original conflict with, as it might start the fight all over again. Choose someone with whom you have a low-conflict relationship.

Phase One: Explore the other person's viewpoint.

Phase Two: Explain your viewpoint.

Phase Three: Create resolutions.

Phase One: Explore the Other Person's Viewpoint

1. Establish that your immediate goal is mutual understanding, not problem-solving.

2. Elicit the other person's thoughts, feelings, and desires about the subject at hand.

3. Ask for the other person's help in understanding him or her. Try not to defend or disagree.

4. Repeat the other person's position in your own words to show you understand.

5. Ask the other person to correct your understanding and keep restating his or her position.

6. Refer back to your position only to keep things going.

7. Repeat steps 1 through 6 until the other person unreservedly agrees that you understand his or her position.

In your notebook or journal, describe a scenario where you engaged in conflict with someone else, and apply the seven steps in Phase One. In other words, write out specifically what you could have asked them to find out what their viewpoint was. For example, "You feel that after you've had a long week at work, you want to relax at the pub for a bit before coming home. Is that correct?" Be careful to leave any tone or negative emotion out of your questioning.

Phase Two: Explain Your Viewpoint

1. Ask for a fair hearing in return.

2. Begin with an explanation of how the other person's thoughts and feelings affect you. Avoid blaming and self-defense as much as possible.

3. Carefully explain your thoughts, desires, and feelings as *your* truth, not *the* truth.

4. Ask for restatements of your position—and corrections of any factual inaccuracies—as necessary.

5. Review your respective positions.

Next, in your notebook or journal, write out how you would explain your position in the scenario you described in Phase One. Be sure to use language that reflects that the frame is yours, and refrain from defending your position as the truth. For example, "For me, after I've had a long week at work, the one person I want to spend time with is you. It's a nice way to kick off the weekend. Can you see my position?"

Phase Three: Create Resolutions

1. Affirm your mutual understanding and confirm that
    you are both ready to consider options for resolution.

2. Brainstorm multiple options.

3. If a mutually agreeable solution is not yet obvious, try
    one or more of the following options:
    - Take time out to reconsider, consult, exchange
      proposals, and reconvene.
    - Agree to neutral arbitration, mediation, or
      counseling.
    - Compromise between alternate solutions.
    - "Take turns" between alternate solutions.
    - Yield (for now) once your position is thoroughly
      and respectfully considered.
    - Assert your positional power after thoroughly
      and respectfully considering their position.
    - Agree to disagree and still respect each other;
      then, if you can, go your separate ways on the
      particular issue.

In your notebook or journal, brainstorm several alternative
solutions to the scenario you've been using in this section.
If you're role-playing with another person, see what innovative ideas they come up with.

Conflict Styles

The Lion. This style is competitive. They value "winning the point" more than the relationship. They see conflict as a competition. "I know they'll come around once they see my point." It's an "I win/you lose" position.

The Ostrich. This style avoids conflict at all costs. To them, having conflict IS the problem, and it's not worth the trouble to argue, because it won't affect the outcome anyway. "I'd rather just forget it." This is an "I lose/you lose" position.

The Dog. This style values the relationship above all else and will accommodate to the other person's desires for the sake of maintaining the relationship. It's the exact opposite of the Lion. "Fine, we'll just do it your way." It's an "I lose/you win" approach.

The Fish. Like a school of fish, this style focuses on collaboration and working together. They want to explore the different options in order to come up with one where everyone benefits. It's an "I win/you win" approach.

The Chameleon. This is the person who adopts the other styles momentarily, in order to communicate with someone with another style.

In your notebook or journal, answer the following questions.

1. Whom do you know that has a Lion style of conflict?

2. Whom do you know that has an Ostrich style of conflict?

3. Whom do you know that has a Dog style of conflict?

4. Whom do you know that has a Fish style of conflict?

5. Give an example of a time when you, or someone else, adopted the Chameleon style.

6. What is your primary style?

7. What is your backup style?

POX Balance Theory

There are four sets of relationships that are usually *balanced*:

- P + O, P + X, O + X
- P – O, P – X, O + X
- P – O, P + X, O – X
- P+O, P – X, O – X

There are also four typically *unbalanced* relationships that are likely to be turned into the above balanced relationships:

- P + O, P – X, O + X
- P + O, P + X, O – X
- P – O, P + X, O + X
- P – O, P – X, O – X

You're watching a television commercial when an actor comes on and offers a testimonial for a politician. In your notebook or journal, write out the POX formula for each of the following situations. You are P. The actor is O. The politician is X.

1. You like both the actor and the politician.

2. You don't like the actor, but you do like the politician.

3. You don't like either the actor or the politician.

4. You like the actor, but not the politician.

How would you tend to react under each of those circumstances?

> *Peace is not the absence of conflict but the*
> *presence of creative alternatives for responding*
> *to conflict—alternatives to passive or aggressive*
> *responses, alternatives to violence.*
> —DOROTHY THOMPSON

PART FOUR

Effective Listening Techniques

9. THE EINSTEIN FACTOR:
Never Stop Questioning

The important thing is to never stop questioning.
—ALBERT EINSTEIN

The Emperor's Three Questions
(from Leo Tolstoy)

One day it occurred to a certain emperor that if he only knew the answers to three questions, he would never stray in any matter.

1. What is the best time to do each thing?

2. Who are the most important people to work with?

3. What is the most important thing to do at all times?

The emperor issued a decree throughout his kingdom announcing that whoever could answer the questions would receive a great reward. Many who read the decree made their way to the palace at once, each person with a different answer.

In reply to the first question, one person advised that the emperor make up a thorough time schedule, consecrating every hour, day, month, and year for certain tasks and then follow the schedule to the letter. Only then could he hope to do every task at the right time.

Another person replied that it was impossible to plan in advance and that the emperor should put all vain amusements aside and remain attentive to everything in order to know what to do at what time.

Someone else insisted that, by himself, the emperor could never hope to have all the foresight and competence necessary to decide when to do each and every task. What he really needed was to set up a council of the wise and then to act according to their advice.

Someone else said that certain matters require immediate decision and could not wait for consultation. If the emperor wanted to know in advance what was going to happen, he should consult magicians and soothsayers.

The responses to the second question also lacked accord.

One person said that the emperor needed to place all his trust in administrators, another urged reliance on priests and monks, while others recommended physicians. Still others put their faith in warriors.

The third question drew a similar variety of answers.

Some said science was the most important pursuit. Others insisted on religion. Yet others claimed the most important thing was military skill.

The emperor was not pleased with any of the answers, and no reward was given.

After several nights of reflection, the emperor resolved to visit a hermit who lived on a mountain and was said to be an enlightened man. The emperor wished to find the hermit to ask him the three questions, though he knew the hermit never left the mountains and was known to receive only the poor, refusing to have anything to do with persons of wealth or power. So the emperor disguised himself as a simple peasant and ordered his attendants to wait for him at the foot of the mountain while he climbed the slope alone to seek the hermit.

Reaching the holy man's dwelling place, the emperor found the hermit digging a garden in front of his hut. When the hermit saw the stranger, he nodded his head in greeting and continued to dig. The labor was obviously hard on him. He was an old man, and each time he thrust his spade into the ground to turn the earth, he heaved heavily.

The emperor approached him and said, "I have come here to ask your help with three questions: When is the best time to do each thing? Who are the most important people to work with? What is the most important thing to do at all times?"

The hermit listened attentively, but only patted the emperor on the shoulder and continued digging. The emperor said, "You must be tired. Here, let me give you a hand with that." The hermit thanked him, handed the emperor the spade, and then sat down on the ground to rest.

After he had dug two rows, the emperor stopped and turned to the hermit and repeated his three questions. The hermit still did not answer, and instead stood and pointed to the spade and said, "Why don't you rest now? I can take over again." The emperor continued to dig. One hour passed, then two. Finally the sun began to set behind the mountain. The emperor put down the spade and said to the hermit, "I came here to ask if you could answer my three questions. If you can't give me any answer, please let me know so that I can get on my way home."

The hermit lifted his head and asked the emperor, "Do you hear someone running over there?" The emperor turned his head. They both saw a man with a long white beard emerge from the woods. He ran wildly, pressing his hands against a bloody wound in his stomach. The man ran toward the emperor before falling unconscious to the ground, where he lay groaning. Opening the man's clothing, the emperor and the hermit saw that the man had received a deep gash. The emperor cleaned the wound thoroughly and then used his own shirt to bandage it, but the blood completely soaked it within minutes. He rinsed the shirt out and bandaged the wound a second time and continued to do so until the flow of blood had stopped.

At last the wounded man regained consciousness and asked for a drink of water. The emperor ran down to the stream and brought back a jug of fresh water. Meanwhile, the sun had disappeared, and the night air had begun to turn cold. The hermit gave the emperor a hand in carrying the man into the hut, where they laid him down on the hermit's bed. The man closed his eyes and lay quietly. The emperor was worn out from a long day of climbing the mountain and digging the garden. Leaning against the doorway, he fell asleep. When he rose, the sun had already risen over the mountain. For a moment he forgot where he was and what he had come here for. He looked over to the bed and saw the wounded man also looking around him in confusion. When he saw the emperor, he stared at him intently and then said in a faint whisper, "Please forgive me."

"What have you done that I should forgive you?" the emperor asked.

"You do not know me, your majesty, but I know you. I was your sworn enemy, and I had vowed to take vengeance on you, for during the last war you killed my brother and seized my property. When I learned that you were coming alone to the mountain to meet the hermit, I resolved to surprise you on your way back and kill you. After waiting a long time there was still no sign of you, and so I left my ambush in order to seek you out. Instead of finding you, I came across your attendants, who recognized me, giving me this wound. Luckily, I escaped and ran here. If I hadn't met you I would surely be dead by now. I had intended to kill you. Instead you saved my life! I am ashamed and grateful beyond words. If I live, I vow to be your servant for the rest of my life, and I will bid my children and grand-children to do the same. Please grant me your forgiveness."

The emperor was overjoyed to see that he was so easily reconciled with a former enemy. He not only forgave the man, but also promised to return all the man's property and to send his own physician and servants to wait on the man until he was completely healed. After ordering his attendants to take the man home, the emperor returned to see the hermit. Before returning to the palace, the emperor wanted to repeat his three questions one last time. He found the hermit sowing seeds in the earth they had dug the day before.

The hermit stood up and looked at the emperor. "Your questions have already been answered."

"How's that?" the emperor asked, puzzled.

"Yesterday, if you had not taken pity on my age and given me a hand with digging these beds, you would have been attacked by that man on your way home. Then you would have deeply regretted not staying with me. Therefore the most important time was the time you were digging in the beds, the most important person was myself, and the most important pursuit was to help me.

"Later, when the wounded man ran up here, the most important time was the time you spent dressing his wound, for if you had not cared for him he would have died and you would have lost the chance to be reconciled with him. Likewise, he was the most important person, and the most important pursuit was taking care of his wound.

"Remember that there is only one important time, and that is now. The present moment is the only time over which we have dominion. The most important person is always the person you are with, who is right before you, for who knows if you will have dealings with any other person in the future? The most important pursuit is making the person standing at your side happy, for that alone is the pursuit of life."

The Question Staircase

This short story is profound for several reasons. First, it illustrates the power of the different kinds of questions we ask. It illustrates the power of listening and being present with the one you are communicating with. And, of course, it illustrates the power of asking meaningful questions and then listening for the answer.

This chapter will establish a model called the Question Staircase, which is a way that allows a listener to ask questions to elicit increasingly meaningful interactions.

The Question Staircase is comprised of three different types of questions. Here is an illustration.

Elementary Questions are often closed-ended questions (meaning that they elicit a brief, factual answer). These questions determine basic information. Examples include:

"When do you need this by?"
"Who will be making the final decision?"
"How do you currently do this process?"

Elaborative Questions are usually open-ended (meaning that they elicit commentary rather than just a simple answer). These questions are intended to elaborate on the basic information we've already obtained by encouraging the person to explain the significance of the information.

"What will it mean if you are able to . . ."
"How do you feel this will affect your department?"
"Which of the issues you've listed is most urgent?"

Evaluative Questions allow the other person to share their thoughts and opinions. They are the most useful for eliciting meaningful communication.

"How does that sound to you?"
"Have I addressed your concern?"
"How would you use this to your benefit?"

Often people will answer the question they think you are asking instead of the one you're really asking.

In the short story presented at the opening of the chapter, one of the problems was that when the emperor asked the questions originally, the people in the kingdom misunderstood what kind of question he was asking. They thought he was asking Elementary Questions ("Who are the most important people to work with?" "Administrators").

The Emperor thought he was asking Elaborative Questions ("What is the most important pursuit?"). The hermit understood that the emperor was really asking an Evaluative Question, and therefore gave him a meaningful answer ("The most important pursuit is making the person standing at your side happy, for that alone is the pursuit of life").

Listening Mistakes

To ensure that you are asking and answering the right type of question for the circumstance, there are several *listening mistakes* to avoid, based on how deeply you're attentive to the other person.

Initial listening takes place when we hear the first few words someone says and then immediately start thinking about what we want to say in return. We then look for a point at which we can interrupt. We are not listening then, because we are spending more time rehearsing what we are going to say about their initial point.

Selective listening means listening for particular things and ignoring others. We hear what we want to hear and don't pay attention to anything else.

False listening occurs when someone pretends to listen without really hearing what's said. A false listener might nod and smile in all the right places without actually taking anything in. We saw an example of this in chapter three, with Leah. However, false listening isn't necessarily a bad thing. It's a skill that may be very useful for people who have to do a great deal of inconsequential listening. Politicians are a good example. When someone is speaking to them, their goal might be to make a good impression in a very short space of time and then move on. They'll never encounter that person again. But if you are trying to elicit a meaningful interaction, false listening should be avoided.

Partial listening is what most of us do most of the time. We listen to the other person with good intentions and then become distracted. Then we dip inside our own heads before starting to listen again. That can be problematic when the other person has moved on and we can't pick up the thread of the conversation. It can also be embarrassing if the other person suddenly asks for your opinion or your advice. If you find this has happened, the best course is to just admit that you had lost the thread of the conversation. Politely ask the other person to repeat what was said.

Full listening happens when the listener pays close and careful attention to the speaker. It means seeking carefully to understand the full content that the other person is trying to convey. This is a very active form of listening, with pauses for summaries and testing that everything is understood. Full listening takes much more effort than partial listening. It requires concentration for a protracted period of time.

Deep listening is a level that not only hears what is said, but also seeks to understand the whole person behind the words. To listen deeply, you need to pay attention not just to the words but also to the whole person who's speaking them. It's difficult to convince people that you respect them just by telling them so. You're much more likely to get this message across by really acting with respect. Deep listening does that most effectively.

Communications Shutdowns

There are certain phrases that can instantly shut down communication between two people. Here is a list of several of them.

1. Don't be ridiculous.
2. It'll cost too much.
3. That's not my responsibility.
4. We don't have time.
5. We've never done that before.
6. That's not the way we do things around here.
7. If it ain't broke, don't fix it.
8. We're not ready for that.
9. You can't teach an old dog new tricks.
10. It will never sell.
11. We will become the laughingstock of the entire company.
12. We tried that before and it didn't work.
13. It simply can't be done.
14. It's too radical a change.
15. That will make our current equipment obsolete.
16. It's not really our problem.

17. Let's get back to reality.
18. Let's form a committee to decide.
19. I need to go over the numbers again.
20. It's not in our budget.
21. We have done all right without it all this time.
22. It won't work here.
23. OK . . . if it doesn't work, you're the one who's going to get the blame.
24. I don't personally agree . . . if you insist.
25. Are you crazy?

If you find yourself saying any of these, stop. The other person is likely to feel "unheard." If someone says these things to you, however, you can probe a little to see if you can break the communication shutdown.

Response Generators

In order to move up the Question Staircase and make sure that you are remaining engaged in the listening process, you can use the following response generators to get the other person to open up and talk more. These would be particularly useful in response to any of the communication shutdown statements.

• Oh?
• In what way?
• How so?
• Tell me more.
• Give me an example.

When you ask these questions, the other person is then prompted to move from Elementary Questions to Evaluative Questions, and from Evaluative Questions to Elaborative Questions.

The Innerview

Gaining a deeper understanding of others allows us to more effectively listen to them, and the best way to do that is to ask meaningful questions. Dale Carnegie Training has developed a technique, called an *Innerview*, which is a series of questions designed to allow a listener to ask effective questions. In this process, there are three basic categories of questions.

Factual Questions. Questions of a typical conversational nature that revolve around factual information.

• Where did you grow up?
• Where did you go to school?
• How did the two of you meet?

Causative Questions. These determine the motive or causative factors behind some of the answers to the factual questions.

• What caused your parents to move there?
• Why did you pick that particular school?
• How did you come to work here?

Values-Based Questions. these will allow you to better understand their frame.

- Tell me about a person who had a major impact on your life.
- If you had it to do over again, what would you do differently?
- What was the toughest part of your life? What got you through?

Gaining a deeper understanding of others allows us to more effectively listen to them, and the best way to do that is to ask meaningful questions.

Questions And Answers

Now it's time to practice what we've learned. Using the following guide, determine what kind of questions follow. The answers are at the bottom of the page.*

    Elementary
    Evaluative
    Elaborative
    Factual
    Causative
    Values-Based

---

* a. Factual. b. Causative. c. Evaluative. d. Values-Based. e. Elementary. f. Elaborative.

a. "What time is the meeting?"
b. "How did you get a flat tire?"
c. "Do you prefer the blue or the red?"
d. "Why did you become a vegetarian?"
e. "What's the process for ordering replacement parts?"
f. "Which car gave you a smoother ride?"

This has been an information-packed chapter, and for good reason. The questions we ask come from the frame by which we see the world. In order to effectively listen, and get inside another person's frame, we've got to be able to ask meaningful and appropriate questions.

In the next chapter, we'll get into an equally informative subject: listening through body language.

Asking questions is what brains were born to do,
at least when we were young children. For young
children, quite literally, seeking explanations is
as deeply rooted a drive as seeking food or water.
—ALISON GOPNIK

10. POKER FACE

There are four ways, and only four ways,
in which we have contact with the world. We are
evaluated and classified by these four contacts:
what we do, how we look, what we say,
and how we say it.
—DALE CARNEGIE

Robert, a former police officer, is about to meet his daughter's boyfriend for the first time. Emily is sixteen, and her boyfriend, Joey, is turning eighteen in a few months. Joey has met Emily's mother, Wendy, several times, but this is the first time he's meeting Robert.

Wendy and Emily have been going on and on all day about how nice Joey is and how much he's looking forward to meeting Robert. "We'll see about that" is all Robert says. He's more than just a protective father. He's also schooled in interpreting nonverbal body language.

The doorbell rings, and Robert answers.

"Hi Mr. Stevenson. I'm Joey. Nice to meet you." Joey extends his hand for a handshake, and then smiles broadly at Robert.

"Come on in, son. Have a seat."

Joey struts over to the couch, and then sits down and

crosses one leg over another, draping one arm over the couch.

He seems pretty confident, thinks Robert. "So tell me a little about yourself, Joey. How are your grades in school?"

Joey's voice remains steady as he answers. "Good, good. I was on the dean's list last semester." Joey's eyebrows rise as he says it, and he starts rubbing his fingers together.

Interesting. He wasn't showing any signs of stress before I asked him about his grades, Robert mentally notes.

"Have you had any serious girlfriends before Emily?"

Joey leans forward in his seat, runs his hands through his hair, and answers, "Uh . . . no. Not really. I had one girlfriend my freshman year, Tiffany. It didn't last long. I'm more interested in school." Joey then licks his lips, and his lips disappear after he is finished talking.

The kid is getting more and more nervous. Let's see if he's just scared of me, or if maybe he wasn't being truthful about his grades or other girlfriends.

"Are you going to watch the big game this weekend? I'm glad our team made the playoffs."

Joey laughs a little, and leans back, and his body relaxes. "Yeah. My dad has a party every year. The whole family comes over for it. In fact, I was going to invite Emily. With your permission, of course . . . sir."

Just then Emily and Wendy walk in the room. "Enough talking, you two. Emily and Joey are going to be late for the movie!"

As the two teenagers walk out the front door, Wendy touches her husband's arm and says, "What did I tell you? Isn't he a nice boy?"

Maybe, Robert thinks. *There were some warning signs, though. I'm going to keep a close eye on him, just to be sure.*

Listening Without Words

It's been said that only 7% of what we communicate is based on the words we speak, 38% of what we communicate is based on voice inflections, and 55% of what we communicate is based on nonverbal behavior. While the numbers may vary depending on the source, it's clear that we can do a lot of listening just by observing things other than a person's words.

In the scenario above, Joey gave off some clear signals about when he was comfortable and uncomfortable. Robert was able to "see through" Joey's words and listen to what Joey was communicating nonverbally. He knew what to look for through observation.

Nonverbal communication is anything that communicates that is not a word.

Ten Cardinal Rules
of Observation

In his book *What Every Body is Saying: An Ex-FBI Agent's Guide to Speed-Reading people,* former FBI agent and body language expert Joe Navarro gives ten cardinal rules of observation to use when you're listening to nonverbal communication.

1. You have to be a competent observer. This means you have to look around and observe the world around you constantly.

2. You have to observe all nonverbal communications in context. The context comes from the totality of what's going on in this person's life.

3. It's important to determine whether a behavior is coming from the brain or is cultural.

4. Are the behaviors unique to this individual? Most people have certain behaviors that they engage in repeatedly.

5. If you're looking at nonverbal communications that are indicative of thoughts, feelings, or intentions, it's best to look for clusters of behaviors rather than relying on one thing.

6. Ask yourself, "What is normal behavior for this person or in this situation?"

7. Also ask yourself, "What behaviors are a change from normal?"

8. Focus on primacy. That is, look for the most immediate expressions as being the most accurate, and use that information as you analyze nonverbal communication.

9. The observations that we make should be nonintrusive.

10. Any time you see a behavior, if you're not sure what it means, always put it into one of two columns. Does it fit within *comfort*, or does it fit within *discomfort*? It's either going to be a comfort display or a discomfort display.

In our opening scenario, Robert needed to determine whether or not Joey's display of certain behaviors was due to the normal discomfort one would feel in meeting one's girlfriend's parents, or if it was related to specific topics, like his grades or previous girlfriends. While signs of discomfort in these areas doesn't automatically mean Joey is lying, it's definitely a red flag for Robert. In this case, Robert used a neutral question—about the big game—to gauge Joey's general comfort level.

Body Talk

Because such a huge part of listening involves observing nonverbal signals, it's helpful to know what to notice. Again, it's important to take these items within the context of the ten cardinal rules.

Here are some interesting things you can look for to tell when someone is comfortable or uncomfortable in their communication with you.*

---

* These are derived from Joe Navarro's book, *What Every Body is Saying: An Ex-FBI's Guide to Speed-Reading People* (New York: William Morrow, 2008).

Feet

Our feet can be indicators of emotion. For example, when a person is standing and they plant one foot on their heel and they point that foot straight up into the air, so the toes are straight up in the air, it's an indication of very positive emotions. If a person is tapping their foot, they are impatient or nervous.

The feet are also indicators of intention. Let's say you're talking to someone and suddenly they start pointing one foot at the door. This is an extremely accurate intention cue of the message, "I've got to go."

Legs

When we cross our legs, this is usually an indication of comfort. It's a comfort display, and we see it around people who genuinely like each other. In our scenario before, Joey crossed his legs because he wasn't feeling very nervous at the time. He uncrossed them when he became uncomfortable with Robert's line of questioning.

Arms

One of the most powerful ways we use our arms is what's called *arms akimbo*. Most of the time, when you see someone standing there with their hands on their hips, elbows out, their legs are slightly spread apart, this is a very territorial display. This is what we see when someone is in charge, when someone's in command. It's a very commanding presence. It can also indicate a problem with the situation.

If you're trying to convey that you are interested and

open, however, change the position of your hands so that your thumbs are facing the speaker.

Crossing the arms can have both a positive connotation and a negative one. To determine which it is, you have to look at the grip. When people are talking to each other and their arms are crossed, and they're gripping their arms very tightly, it's usually indicative of something very negative.

Otherwise, it isn't necessarily associated with something negative. One can have one's arms crossed, leaning back on a chair, and be very relaxed. When we are in a social setting where there are other people around us, we derive a certain amount of comfort putting our hands across our chest.

At times when we want to create a psychological barrier, we'll place an object like a pillow or a blanket or a coat over our arms or torso.

Hands

The hands are one of the best places to look for nonverbal messages. In our example in the opening, Joey engaged Robert in a firm handshake. A firm handshake is a sign of dominance and aggression. A flaccid handshake is an indication of shyness. Women who have a strong handshake are indicating that they are open to new experiences. The same correlation isn't true for men. Superiors tend to have firmer handshakes than their subordinates, and friends exert equal pressure when shaking hands. Therefore, when Joey shook Robert's hands as equals, it was a bit of a red flag to Robert. This was an imbalanced power situation, and Joey's overly firm handshake indicated that he might be trying too hard to appear confident.

Also, a quick handshake indicates a lack of interest or enthusiasm. A slightly longer than normal handshake is a sign of dominance.

When we love each other—when we hold a child, when we hold someone that's dear to us—we tend to touch them with the full palms of our hands. Our skin fully touches this individual, whether it's your mother, your grandmother, or the loving face of a child. So if someone is saying they love you, look to see if they are touching you open-handed.

Another thing the hands can tell us is *precision*. When we put our fingers together, the thumb and the first two fingers, we can indicate precision.

We can talk about something expansive by using *jazz hands*—where we extend our fingers fully and they stretch, and we are transported to something different when we use expressive hands. You'll note that politicians do this a lot.

Steepling is when we bring our fingertips together but don't allow our palms to touch, so that our fingers look like a church steeple. Steepling is in fact the most powerful behavior that we have to show confidence. It shows that we're very confident about what we're talking about.

Steepling is the most powerful behavior that we have to show confidence.

Shoulders

Imagine a teenager being asked the question, "Is your brother home from school yet?" She brings one shoulder up to the ear and says, "I don't know." Now contrast that with her being asked, "Is your brother home from school yet?" This time both shoulders come up to the ears, her palms up, and she says, "I don't know." Which is more believable?

Neck

The neck is one of those places we tend to touch in order to soothe ourselves when we are under stress. Massaging the back of the neck while speaking is a classic indicator of discomfort.

When women feel insecure, when they're distressed, when they're troubled or feel threatened, they'll cover a little area called the *suprasternal notch*—the large, visible dip between the neck and the collarbone—with the tips of their fingers or with their hands.

Head

This is another area where you can observe if someone is listening to you or convey to someone that you're listening to them. You're talking to someone, and at some point in the conversation, your head begins to comfortably tilt as you're listening to them. If something is mentioned that you don't particularly care for, your head will immediately straighten up.

Forehead

The forehead is one of the easiest places on the body to see anxiety. It presents us, in real time, with a very accurate picture of a person's thoughts and feelings. It can easily and clearly show us when there is stress, when there is comfort, when things are not going the right way, or when something is troubling us. In our scenario above, Joey's eyebrows went up, and his forehead indicated that he was anxious about what he was saying. That, combined with his leaning forward and his running his hands through his hair to self-soothe, alerted Robert to the fact that Joey was not comfortable with the conversation.

Eyes

While most people think of blinking the eyes merely as a way to lubricate them, it's actually a very effective blocking mechanism. Most of the time when we hear something we don't like, we actually close our eyes. Sometimes it's just for a tenth of a second, sometimes it's for a little longer, but it's one of the blocking mechanisms that the human brain has found to protect itself.

Many times when you hear bad news, or you are being told of something that stresses you, you'll find yourself closing your eyes as you are processing this information. So if someone is listening to you, and they close their eyes, it might not be that they aren't listening. It might be that they don't like what you're telling them.

Eyebrows

This is one of the classic comical gestures to indicate interest: a man looks at a woman, nods his head, and makes his eyebrows go up, as if to say, "How you doin'?" This is called the *eyebrow flash*, and is a sign of comfort or interest.

Imagine meeting someone and, as you go to shake their hand, their eyes are just fixed, and then you meet another person and as you go to shake their hand, they look at you and they arch their eyebrows the eyebrow flash. Which indicates more attention to you?

Mouth

When we have a true, sincere smile, the muscles around the eyes are engaged in the process. In a true smile, the corners of the mouth come up towards the eyes and the eyes will reflect the smile, because the muscles of the eyes will be involved in it. Unfortunately, this is also where we get the crow's feet effect.

The false smile—the social smile—is the smile that moves the corners of the mouth towards the ears but does not involve the eyes. This is one way to assess genuine emotions. When Robert was meeting Joey, and Joey gave him a broad smile, Robert looked to see if the smile went all the way to the boy's eyes. If so, then it meant he was genuinely looking forward to meeting Robert. If not, he was giving a false smile to give a positive impression.

Also remember that at one point in the conversation, Joey's lips seemed to disappear. The lips disappear because of the high degree of stress that the person is undergoing.

It has nothing to do with deception. It has nothing to do with truth or lying. When you see lips that have disappeared, there's a high degree of stress. Lip tension indicates mental tension, and when the corners of the mouth turn downward, then emotions are really low.

Biting the lip and cheek can have different connotations as well. This is why it's so important to keep these observations in context. For example, George W. Bush used to bite the inside of his cheek when he was highly nervous or anxious, and Bill Clinton had a tendency to bite his lower lip as a way of demonstrating his sincerity.

Chin

We've all seen the classic professor or therapist move—touching the chin or stroking a beard (real or imaginary). Chin touching is associated with pensiveness, with thinking, with thought, and with precision of ideas.

This gesture is to be differentiated from that of people who touch their faces, especially around the jaw line. We tend to pacify ourselves by touching our jaws, and we tend to show we're thinking of something by touching a little narrow area that is about two inches wide on the chin. In our scenario above, Joey touched his jaw here when Robert's line of questioning made him nervous.

So when you see someone touching their chin as they're walking or sitting, it's doesn't mean that they are pacifying themselves, but rather that they're thinking. If they're touching their jaw, that's more likely to be pacifying.

The jaw can also tell us about confidence or insecurity. When we're strong and confident, our jaw comes out. When we are weak and insecure, and when we lack confidence, we tuck our chin in.

A blur of blinks, taps, jiggles,
pivots and shifts . . . the body language
of a man wishing urgently to be elsewhere.
—EDWARD R. MURROW

Preening

We see it all over the animal kingdom. Animals preen as an effort to make themselves look attractive to the opposite sex. Humans are animals too, but instead of fluffing our feathers, we adjust our hair, glasses, or jewelry, or straighten our ties.

Preening in this manner sends a very powerful message to the other people who are in your presence. It subconsciously conveys to them, "You're important enough for me to spend this energy to put myself together to preen for you." There are also negative preening behaviors, particularly when one person starts to preen another. We see it in movies. A bad guy is trying to intimidate someone. He starts picking lint off the other person's clothes or adjusts his glasses. It's a sign of disrespect, and when the other person allows it to continue, it's a strong statement of not having power in the situation.

Pacifying

We tend to think of pacifying as something that babies do to calm themselves down, such as sucking their thumb or twirling their hair. Although we do see it in young children, pacifying behaviors continue on in adulthood as well. Here are some examples. When you see a person doing this, it means that they are feeling anxious.

- Rubbing the forehead
- Pulling on hair
- Rubbing the nose
- Massaging the nose
- Pulling on the upper lip
- Stroking the chin
- Massaging the ears
- Pulling on the earlobes
- Twirling a pencil
- Mangling a paperclip
- Playing with a rubber band
- Rubbing their fingers
- Playing with jewelry (twisting a ring or pulling on a necklace)

Using Nonverbal Communication to Convey Listening

Much of what we've covered here is how you can use observations of nonverbal communication to listen to what a speaker is saying, beyond words.

You can also use it to let the other person know that you are listening to them.

When listening, you can use nonverbal communication to SOFTEN the position of others. SOFTEN stands for:

S = Smile
O = Open posture
F = Forward lean
T = Touch
E = Eye contact
N = Nod

In this chapter, we've covered how important observation of body language is to listening.

In the next chapter, we'll discuss this problem: how can you accurately "listen" to another person when you are not in their physical presence?

11. LISTENING IN THE NEW MILLENNIUM

Social media is just a platform. Twitter is a very simple and immediate broadcast platform. Facebook is a very personal, when it comes to friends and when it comes to fan pages, a little bit less but still somewhat personal way to communicate.
—MARK CUBAN

Hey Rob. So, I wanted to let you know that Chris and I have started dating, and it's getting pretty serious.

You mean Chris, my college roommate? The one I introduced you to on New Year's, when you were my GIRLFRIEND?

Yeah, that Chris. But, listen, you broke up with me, so I didn't think you'd care if he and I started seeing each other. We didn't intend to get serious. It was just hanging out at first.

Rachel, do you remember WHY I broke up with you? I caught you texting my brother!

That was different, and you know it.

Well, congratulations. I'm happy for you both. I hope it works out for you.

Thanks Rob! I knew you'd understand. ☺

Written Communication:
The Most Misunderstood Medium

At this point, we've pretty much all had it happen at one time or another. We say or respond to something through a text message or e-mail. The other person misunderstands, and the next thing you know, you're in a huge argument.

The scenario above is just one example. Without the benefit of nonverbal cues and tone differences such as inflection, volume, and pace, it's very easy to misinterpret communications that are coming in written form.

And yet the problem is not going to go away. At the time of this writing, Facebook has 1.71 billion users that are active every month. That's not even counting Twitter, Instagram, and online dating sites. Add in the millions of e-mails and texts that are sent every single day, and it's no wonder written communication is responsible for so much conflict.

Conveying Emotion In Writing

The scenario above illustrates the challenges we face when conveying emotion in writing. Rachel is telling her ex-boyfriend Rob that she has started dating someone he knows. That is the message. Without the contextual clues that we would normally get with a verbal conversation, we don't know her frame. Since her frame affects how she encodes the message, and this is a difficult message to begin with, that's the first opportunity for conflict. What was Rachel's motivation for telling Rob? Is she clueless, or is she being kind and letting him know directly from her before he hears it from someone else? Or has she found out that he's seeing someone else too, and is telling him about Chris for revenge, yet is trying to make it sound sweet?

As we've learned, contextual clues in verbal conversation can allow the receiver to understand the frame of the sender. Without them, it becomes up to the listener to interpret.

Also, as we've learned, the receiver's frame influences how the message is decoded. In our example, Rob demonstrates three different responses that are based on how he has decoded her message. Because she is his ex-girlfriend, and has a history of inappropriate communication with men (remember that if we have a history or repeated interactions with someone, we tend to view ALL of our interactions with them through that frame), he is framing her news negatively.

Heider's Balance Theory* teaches us that if Rob had a positive view of Rachel, then he would more likely be accepting of their relationship.

Friends of Friends

As an example, in an episode of the '90s television show *Friends*, brother and sister characters (Ross and Monica) are having a conversation in which she is telling him that she has fallen in love with their mutual friend Chandler.

At first he is shocked and hurt, and has an angry tone.

---

* https://en.wikipedia.org/wiki/Balance_theory, accessed Aug. 15, 2016.

Ross: My best friend and my sister. I CANNOT BELIEVE THIS!

Monica: I'm sorry, but it's true. I love him too.

Then he realizes how amazing it is that two people he loves are in love with each other too, and his tone changes to happiness.

Ross: My best friend AND my sister! I cannot believe this!

They then all have a group hug.

Now just imagine that that conversation had only taken place over text message or some other written medium. There would be no way for Monica to know how Ross really feels about her relationship with Chandler. She needs to be able to see his body language and hear his vocal intonation.

Without the contextual clues that we would normally get with a verbal conversation, we don't know the other person's frame.

No Test Today

Here's an example you can try yourself. Read the following sentence aloud six different ways:

"We are not going to take a test today."

1. Statement indicating surprise.

2. Statement of fact.

3. Statement indicating that we will be doing something other than taking a test today.

4. Statement indicating that some other group will be taking a test today.

5. Statement indicating we absolutely will not be taking a test today.

6. Statement indicating that we will have more than one test today.

Here are the different ways that emphasis can affect the interpretation of that sentence.

1. Statement indicating surprise: We are not going to take a test today? (Note the question mark.)

2. Statement of fact: We are not going to take a test today. (No inflection or tone.)

3. Statement indicating that we will be doing something other than taking a test today: We are not going to take a test TODAY. (Note emphasis on the word *today*.)

4. Statement indicating that some other group will be taking a test today: WE are not going to take a test today. (Note the emphasis on the word *we*.)

5. Statement indicating we absolutely will not be taking a test today: We are NOT going to take a test today. (Note the emphasis on the word *not*.)

6. Statement indicating that we will have more than one test today: We are not going to take A test today. (Note the emphasis on the word *a*.)

Tone Matters

Here are some ways that you can convey tone (or understand other people's tones) in written communication.

Bolding And All Caps

In our scenario above, Rob uses all caps for emphasis. By capitalizing the words MY GIRLFRIEND, he is emphasizing the fact that she had a pattern of talking to other guys when they were dating. By using all caps, he is, in essence, yelling those words.

Emoticons And Emojis

You've probably already seen *emoticons*—textual pictures of faces—in electronic messages. By far the three most common one are:

:-) *smiley*, which means, "I'm happy."
;-) *winky*, which means, "I'm kidding."
:-(*frowny*, which means, "I'm sad or disappointed."

While there are numerous others, from *ill* (%^P) to *angry* (>:-<) to *astonished* (:-o), these are much less common and so more open to misinterpretation.

Many smartphones have graphic emoticons, called *emojis,* which make it much easier to convey tone. In our scenario above, Rachel used a smiley face to indicate that she was happy with Rob's seeming acceptance of her relationship. (She didn't, however, pick up on his sarcasm.)

Punctuation And Abbreviation

Another way we can convey tone in writing is through the use of punctuation and abbreviation.

You've probably already seen *(?)* to indicate uncertainty or *(sp?)* when someone isn't sure about the spelling of a word:

"What's the name of that consultant we hired?"
"Vujicic (sp?). He's scheduled to arrive next week (?) and start taking surveys."

164 LISTEN! THE ART OF EFFECTIVE COMMUNICATION

While the use of "um . . ." in verbal communication is frowned upon, and is inappropriate in formal communication, it can be useful in casual written communication. It conveys a tone of either surprise or irritation.

"When are you going to call the gardener??"
"Um . . . I did that last week."

Or it can be used to convey that you're not sure.

"How many boxes of staples did you order?"
"Um . . . about seventeen."

Perhaps the most often used abbreviation is *LOL*. It literally stands for "laugh out loud," and was originally used to indicate humor. It has since transitioned to becoming a softener for statements that would otherwise sound harsh. "Don't be late again" sounds very different than "Don't be late again, LOL." The first sounds angry. The second sounds empathetic.

Similarly *(jk)* or "just kidding" is often used when someone is exaggerating or saying something playful. Using softeners like this can go a long way to making sure that your tone is understood.

We Think We're Better Than We Are

Generally speaking, people tend to think they are better at listening to and interpreting tone in written messages than they really are.

According to a study by the *Journal of Personal Social Psychology*, test participants e-mailed ten statements to a recipient. Some statements were serious, some sarcastic. These senders believed the recipient would correctly identify the intended emotion behind most of the messages. In fact, the recipients only identified seriousness or sarcasm 56% of the time, which isn't much better than chance.*

When the same messages were transmitted through a voice recording, the recipient interpreted the emotion correctly 73% of the time, just about what senders expected. Vocal tones captured the emotional nuance that e-mail couldn't. The researchers believe that when people type out a sarcastic line, they hear it in their heads as sarcastic, and thus fail to appreciate that others won't hear it the same way. This, of course, relates to the different frames between sender and receiver.

Here are some tips when communicating via text or e-mail.

- Wait before responding to a message that angers you. Have a trusted friend review any messages you wrote when you were angry to make sure that you're conveying the tone you wish to be conveying.
- Convey emotions with emoticons or emojis, or through actual words "I'm happy to report that . . ."

---

* Justin Kruger et al., "Egocentrism over E-mail: Can We Communicate as Well as We Think?", *Journal of Personality and Social Psychology* 89:5, 925–936.

- All-capital letters and exclamation marks indicate urgency. Use them sparingly.
- Use uncertainty markers to show how confident you are about what you say.

When the Receiver Is You

When you receive a written communication that sounds curt or offensive, take a break before responding. During the break, look at your frame and see how it might be influencing your interpretation. Ask yourself: *can I understand this message in another way?*

Try to think of an alternative frame that is more positive on the part of the sender. Here is an example. Larry and Tracy have plans this weekend, and both of them have been putting in a lot of overtime.

> Larry: Hey, do you want to cancel our plans for the museum tomorrow? You might be tired.

Tracy's initial reaction is that Larry is the one who is actually tired and wants to cancel the plans, but he doesn't want to tell her that, so he's presenting it as being sensitive to her. From that frame, she might write back something like this.

> Tracy: Look, if you're too tired to go, just say so. Don't cancel our plans and pretend you're doing it for me.

But if she sends this message, it's likely to escalate into an argument. So she challenges the assumption that Larry is only PRETENDING to be sensitive to her needs. "What if he really is just trying to be nice?" So she sends the following message instead.

Tracy: "I'm not too tired—thanks for asking. If you're tired, we can cancel though."

The Changing Face of Communication

The bottom line is this: the advent of e-mails, text messages, and social media has changed the way we communicate with each other. In order to effectively "listen" through written communication, we have to become especially attuned to how our own frame influences our interpretation of what we are reading.

My Listening Log
Part Four

The Listening Staircase

Elementary Questions determine basic information.

Elaborative Questions elaborate on the basic information we've already obtained.

Evaluative Questions allow the other person to share their thoughts and opinions.

In your notebook or journal, answer the following questions.

1. Give a recent example of an Elementary Question you asked.

2. Give a recent example of an Elaborative Question you asked.

3. Give a recent example of an Evaluative Question you asked.

Communication Shutdowns

Describe a time when you shut down communication by using one of the communication shutdowns.

Then describe a time when that happened to you.

The Innerview

An Innerview is a series of questions designed to allow a listener to ask effective questions.

Choose a person to practice conducting an Innerview with. Write down your experiences and reflections in your notebook or journal.

Cultural Differences in Body Language

Go out into public and become an observer of cultural and other differences in body language. In your notebook or journal, describe your observations of the following categories of people.

Ethnic/racial norms (e.g., Asians and Australians).
Gender differences (men and women, as well as
    transsexuals or gender-neutral individuals).
Corporate culture (e.g., Whole Foods versus Safeway).
Political groups (e.g., Democrats and Republicans).
Geography (e.g., East Coast versus West Coast).
Income (e.g., millionaires and blue-collar workers).
Religious groups (e.g., Muslims and evangelical Christians).

The SOFTEN Method of Nonverbal Listening

S = Smile
O = Open posture
F = Forward lean
T = Touch
E = Eye contact
N = Nod

Practice this technique at work and in your personal life: choose one person in each situation that you've had challenges with, and then note your observations in your notebook or journal.

Written Communication

In your notebook or journal, answer the following questions.

1. Describe a time when you had an argument over a text message or e-mail.

2. Is there a way that you could have reframed the intent of the other person? (Look up the conversation, if possible.)

3. Could you have used emojis, abbreviations, or softeners to defuse the situation?

CONCLUSION

You can make more friends in two months
by becoming interested in other people
than you can in two years by trying
to get other people interested in you.
—DALE CARNEGIE

Well, there you have it. You've now learned everything you need to know in order to become a more effective listener. We've examined factors that are influenced by the receiver, the message, and the sender, and are now more aware of where listening problems can occur.

Here are several "Myths of Listening" that we've busted in this book.

Myth #1. *Listening means agreeing.* Very often in arguments, people will say, "You're not listening to me!" In truth, what they often mean is, "I can't get you to agree with me!" Listening and agreeing are not the same thing.

Myth #2. *Listening takes a lot of effort and work.* In reality, it only takes about 45 seconds of focused, deep listening for the speaker to feel heard.

Myth #3. *"Acting like you're listening" is the same thing as listening.* Even when a person makes eye contact, mimics body language, repeats back to the person what they just heard, or other "gimmicks" of listening, it's not necessarily true that the person was actually listening. The person might have been planning their response instead of listening.

Myth #4. *Listening takes too much time.* Often it is challenging for a listener to let the other person get his or her point out. You've already figured out what they are going to say and already know what your response is. For example, a child goes to his mother and says, "Mom, this Saturday, after basketball, can I . . . ?" The mother already knows that the child is going to ask to go to a friend's house. She also knows that they have another activity planned and the child cannot go. It's tempting for the mother to interrupt and say, "No, you can't go to Johnny's house, we have to go to Grandma's." Listening is more than hearing the other person's words. It's about making them feel validated. So Mom has to discipline herself to let the child speak fully and without being interrupted, even when she knows what is going to be said.

Becoming a Mindful Listener

A mindful listener is one who understands more than just the content of what is being said. To truly be a mindful listener, one has to observe the attitude, language level, vocal expressions, pauses, nonverbal communication, and other information to get the whole picture.

The mindful listener is able to step back and observe the speaker, even if he is not interested or doesn't agree at all with what the other person is saying. For example, let's say your husband and children are avid video game players, and you have no interest in this hobby whatsoever. Being a mindful listener means stepping back and letting them talk: "And then I scored fourteen golden tokens and went to the Wheel of Wonder, where my avatar . . ." The mindful listener is able to do this by thinking, "Look how happy this makes him. He is so excited about the golden tokens." *She* doesn't care about the tokens; she cares that *he* cares. This makes him feel valued and respected.

Barriers to Mindful Listening

As we've discovered in this book, there are several barriers to mindful listening. While you can't control the frame of another person, you can certainly change your own. Perhaps the easiest way to identify a frame that needs changing is to listen to your own negative self-talk. Many people are listening to their own critical self-talk instead of listening to the speaker. And interestingly, people who have a high level of negative self-talk are more likely to perceive what you are saying in a negative light.

Other barriers to becoming a mindful listener include: wanting to get to one's own agenda; one's past experiences; preoccupation with self-needs; resistance; prejudice; past mistakes; external distraction; and bias and opinions, as well as communication style differences. Those with different styles often have trouble communicating because they aren't able to "hear" in the other style.

Summing Up

While listening is only one side of a conversation, it is often the neglected side. The first step to becoming a better listener is to recognize that effective listening is a dynamic process. It's about understanding your own filters and frames, recognizing the factors that affect the message itself, and challenging your assumptions about the other person's filters and frames.

When you become a better listener, you have the power to change your relationships.

> *When people talk, listen completely.*
> *Most people never listen.*
> —ERNEST HEMINGWAY

Can You Hear Me *Now*?

To discover how much you've learned in this book, retest your listening skills by retaking the following self-assessment quiz.

For the following questions, answer on the following scale. Try to be as honest with yourself as possible.

Not at all   Rarely   Sometimes   Often   Very often

1. When I'm on the phone with someone, it's fine to respond to e-mails and text messages at the same time as long as I'm listening.

2. When listening to another person, I start to get upset and react emotionally.

3. I feel uncomfortable with silence during conversations.

4. If I have a relevant story to share, I'll interrupt the other person to tell it and then get back to letting them talk.

5. People seem to get upset during some conversations with me, and it seems to come out of nowhere.

6. To keep the conversation flowing, I ask questions that can be answered with a simple "yes" or "no" response.

7. I play "devil's advocate" to help the other person see a different side of what they are saying.

8. If someone wants to talk about something over and over again, I'll just tell them what they want to hear to get them to stop.

9. As I listen, I am figuring out what I am going to say back to the other person.

10. I'm uncomfortable when people talk to me about sensitive subjects.

11. If another person has a different view on something I feel strongly about, I don't want to talk about it.

12. I don't really pay much attention to things like the environment or body language. What matters is what the other person is actually saying.

13. If the other person is struggling to say something, I'll fill in with my own suggestions.

14. If I'm interrupted from doing something when someone wants to talk, I feel impatient for them to finish so I can get back to what I was doing.

To determine your score, give yourself the following points for each answer:

Not at all = 1 point
Rarely = 2 points
Sometimes = 3 points
Often = 4 points
Very often= 5 points

Score Interpretation

14–29: Gold Medalist
You've got terrific listening skills already. You've got the ability to make people feel heard and want to talk to you. You're emotionally present and give people your full attention. Strive to continue to grow and evolve.

30–49: Silver Medalist
People enjoy talking to you. Sometimes if subjects get too emotional or uncomfortable, you tend to change the subject or make a joke.

50–70: Bronze Medalist
If you scored in this category, you might think you're a better listener than others do. You might be giving people the feeling that you don't care about what they're saying, or you might have frequent misunderstandings.

INTUITION:
The Art of Listening to Yourself

It is always with excitement that I wake up in the morning wondering what my intuition will toss up to me, like gifts from the sea. I work with it and rely on it. It's my partner.
—JONAS SALK

On September 11, 2001, Greer Epstein did something she rarely did: she took a cigarette break at 8:40 a.m. An executive director at Morgan Stanley, with an office on the sixty-seventh floor of the South Tower of the World Trade Center in New York, she rarely had the time for a smoking break before lunch.

But on this fateful day, a colleague called and wanted to talk about an upcoming work meeting and asked, "How about getting a cigarette?" Greer looked out her window and saw a beautiful morning—perhaps the clearest day she had ever seen from her office. She thought, "Why not?"

While riding down the elevator, she felt a jolt, but dismissed it because the elevators always tended to act up. When she and the colleague stepped outside the building, they saw dozens of people standing and looking toward the sky at a gaping hole in the North Tower.

Still not fully aware of what had happened, she wondered, "How are they ever going to fix that?" It was at that moment that a plane flew directly into her office in the South Tower.

That simple thought "Why not?" saved Greer Epstein's life.

Almost everyone has experienced intuition at one point or another. You're thinking of someone, and they call. You have the urge to take a different route to work, only to find out there was an accident on your normal path. You meet someone and instantly get a gut feeling that they aren't to be trusted. These gut feelings we get are a form of knowing that isn't based on a conscious assessment, but instead arises seemingly out of the blue.

Naval Knowing

A lot of folks consider intuition to be something weird or "woo woo." But the idea that we all have a sixth sense is gaining acceptance in the most unlikely of places—including the U.S. Navy.

The Navy has started a program to investigate how members of the military can be trained to improve their sixth sense, or intuitive ability, during combat and other missions.*

The program developed because so many of the troops in Iraq and Afghanistan were coming back reporting that

---

* Channing Joseph, "U.S. Navy Program to Study How Troops Use Intuition"; *The New York Times*, March 27, 2012; http://atwar.blogs.nytimes.com/2012/03/27/navy-program-to-study-how-troops-use-intuition/?_r=0; accessed Aug. 15, 2016.

they had experienced an unexplained feeling of danger right before an enemy attack.

In an article in *The New York Times*, the Office of Naval Research was quoted as saying, "Research in human pattern recognition and decision-making suggest that there is a 'sixth sense' through which humans can detect and act on unique patterns without consciously and intentionally analyzing them . . .

"Evidence is accumulating that this capability, known as intuition or intuitive decision making, enables the rapid detection of patterns in ambiguous, uncertain and time restricted information contexts."

Intuition is the product of unconscious information processing

---

John Kounios, a professor of psychology at Drexel University, is quoted as saying that when an idea appears as an "aha" moment or as a product of that sixth sense, "people often think that this is a psychic phenomenon because they don't know where the idea came from. But it's the product of unconscious information processing."

Intuition Defined

What exactly *is* intuition, then? Here are a few select definitions from the academic literature.*

---

* Erik Dane and Michael G. Pratt, "Exploring Intuition and Its Role in Managerial Decision Making." *Academy of Management Review* 32:1 (2007): 33–54.

Jung: The psychological function that transmits perceptions in an unconscious way.

Shirley and Langan-Fox: A feeling of knowing with certitude on the basis of inadequate information and without conscious awareness of rational thinking.

Burke and Miller: A cognitive conclusion based on a decisionmaker's previous experiences and emotional inputs.

Lieberman: The subjective experience of a mostly nonconscious process—fast, alogical, and inaccessible to consciousness—that, depending on exposure to the domain or problem space, is capable of accurately extracting probabilistic contingencies.

While there are dozens, if not hundreds, of definitions of intuition, the vast majority of them mention a few defining characteristics.

One characteristic of intuition is that it is *nonconscious*—it occurs outside of conscious thought. It's not so much that you "think" something, you just "sense" or "know" it.

A second characteristic is that intuition involves a process in which environmental stimuli are matched with some deeply held (nonconscious) category, pattern, or feature. This sounds very reminiscent of the frames and filters we have been mentioning throughout this book.

A third characteristic of the intuition process is its *speed*. It's this characteristic that differentiates intuition from other ways of knowing.

What Intuition Is NOT

There are many terms that are almost synonymous with intuition, but aren't the same. If we consider that intuition is nonconscious, then it's not the same thing as *insight*. An insight is understanding that we gain through deliberate and analytical thinking that we then set aside to "incubate." An example of this is an entrepreneur who wants to start a business, so she explores different business opportunities and then later gets a flash of insight that leads her to a choice.

Similarly, intuition is not the same thing as *instinct*. Instinct is a hard-wired mechanism in the brain that causes our bodies and minds to respond automatically to a stimulus. An example is feeling fear when looking over a ledge or a cliff. One doesn't need to have fallen off a ledge to have an instinctive knowing to stay away from it.

The Power of Intuition

If intuition is a matter of unconsciously processing information from the environment around us, then how can we harness its power? What can learning to listen to your intuition do for you?

Imagine being able to get a "feel" for when someone is lying to you. What if you could better know when to trust someone or not? How about being able to trust your choices and decisions, even in the face of rational opposition? Learning to listen to your intuition can do just that.

Intuition comes from the ability to see microexpressions in people's faces and bodies, or slight things in the environment that seem different. Stay in touch with the world, and you start to see patterns. These sensitivities come more naturally to some; some are just more sensitive.

What Blocks Intuition?

Even people with natural abilities can find themselves unable to access their intuition. One thing that contributes to this is being overly busy. If we are rushing from one thing to the next, constantly checking our phones and our social media, texting while walking and driving, we can miss those subtle clues that lead to intuition.

Sometimes, too, we don't WANT to listen. We meet someone who is charming and attractive, and there is this small voice that says something isn't right. But they are just SO attractive, and we choose to ignore the feeling. Then when our hearts have been broken, we look back and say, "I really did know it all along." It's the job you shouldn't have taken, the friend you shouldn't have lent money to, the decision you let someone talk you into.

Another big block to intuition is *negative emotion*. When we are experiencing strong emotions, our brains turn on the sympathetic nervous system, which is a way of minimizing the number of things we can focus on during a crisis. If you're being chased down the street by a bad guy, you're not likely to notice the smell of garlic bread emanating from your favorite Italian restaurant. So when we are angry, depressed, or in a bad mood, our intuition can escape us.

In fact, a 2013 study published in the journal *Psychological Science* showed that being in a positive mood boosted the ability to make intuitive judgments in a word game.*

That's not to say that intuitive people never get upset—but your intuition will fare better if you're able to mindfully accept and let go of negative emotions for the most part, rather than suppressing or dwelling on them.

Eight Ways to Develop your Intuition

What are some ways in which you can learn to develop and trust your intuition? Here are eight ways.

1. *Meditate.* Many people think that meditation is sitting cross-legged on a pillow, chanting. While that is what happens in some forms of meditation, other

---

* Annette Bolte, Thomas Goschke, and Julius Kuhl, "Emotion and Intuition Effects of Positive and Negative Mood on Implicit Judgments of Semantic Coherence," *Psychological Science* 14:5 (Sept. 2003), 416–421; http://pss.sagepub.com/content/14/5/416. short; accessed Aug. 15, 2016.

forms are more like quiet reflection. It's about being still and allowing the thoughts you have to float by like clouds in the sky. Messages from your intuition tend to be quiet, so spending time in silence will help you hear and interpret these messages.

2. *Use your senses.* Since intuition comes from subtle clues in the environment, one way to develop the sixth sense is to develop the other five. What do you hear? How does something taste? Look very closely at things. Smell them. Touch things. Become an observer of life.

3. *Pay attention to your dreams.* When the cognitive mind is busy, it can override the quiet voice of intuition. But when you're sleeping, your cognitive mind rests and your nonconscious mind can send you symbols and messages.

4. *Get creative.* Engaging in creative activities, such as drawing, scrapbooking, or free-flow journaling, quiets the cognitive mind and allows your intuition to speak up.

5. *Take a shower.* Have you ever heard someone say, "I get my best ideas in the shower?" There's something about the feeling of warm running water and the repetitive motion of bathing that quiets the conscious mind and allows creativity to flow. If you're trying to access your intuition, take a shower or do the dishes.

6. *Observe people.* See what kind of information you can glean from observing people before you talk to them or learn anything about them from other people. The more you pay attention, the more you'll realize you already know things you couldn't possibly know with the cognitive mind.

7. *Align with your values.* Your mind may steer you away from your integrity, but your intuition never will. If something "feels" wrong, it probably is.

8. *Practice the listening techniques in this book.* Just as you can use the ideas and techniques in this book to become a better listener to others, you can use them to learn to listen to your intuition. As an old joke says, "I talk to myself because I'm the only one who always thinks I'm right!"

> *I believe in intuitions and inspirations . . .*
> *I sometimes FEEL that I am right.*
> *I do not KNOW that I am.*
> —Albert Einstein

FOURTEEN DAYS
TO BETTER LISTENING

OK, so you've read the book and looked or worked through the exercises. Now it's time to put the pedal to the metal and really start to apply what you've learned. It's not about becoming the perfect listener overnight. Research shows that people who make small changes are far more likely to keep those changes than those who try to overhaul their lives. This chapter will give you a solid plan with practical things you can start doing today to become a better listener in fourteen days. Sometimes when you make a lot of tiny changes, you look around and find that they added up to significant improvement!

Of course your work life and your home life are not mutually exclusive. They spill over onto each other. So when you become a better listener at work, you naturally become a better listener at home.

We're starting with your workplace first, because that is usually less emotionally charged than your home life. You'll have a week to practice your listening skills before moving on to the home arena.

Let's get started!

Week One: Better Listening at Work: Bosses, Peers, Subordinates, and Others

Day 1: The Detective

Today you are going to become an undercover detective at work—observing other people. Knowing what you know now after reading this book, who are the effective listeners in your workplace? Write their names in the following space, along with an example of them engaging in effective listening. Try and come up with five.

1.

2.

3.

4.

5.

Now write down the names of those you observe who are *not* engaging in effective listening. What are they doing that you now know is a sign of poor listening? Again, try to come up with five.

1.

2.

3.

4.

5.

Which of the behaviors, both positive and negative, do you want to work on? In other words, which effective listening behaviors do you want to increase, and which do you want to decrease or eliminate?

Day 2: Frames and Filters at Work

As you go through your day, reflect on how your frames and filters affect your listening.

YOUR BOSS

Describe an interaction with your boss that happened today. You most likely heard him or her through the "boss/employee" filter. In other words, what information did you focus on the most when communicating with this person, and what do you leave out? Describe what you heard based on your filter.

Now shift the frame a little bit. Think of your boss as an employee, for example. Now how do you hear what he or she said? Does the frame shift affect your perception of the interaction? Write your observations here:

Day 3: Unconscious Biases

YOUR CO-WORKERS

As mentioned in the book, unconscious biases tend to influence communication. See if you can observe an inter-action with a co-worker where one of you was somehow biased. This is not necessarily a racial bias—but is one where the person's view of things influences how they hear messages. For example, Sally hears that Mark got approved for overtime. She believes that he always gets approved for overtime because he doesn't work hard enough during the day. Write down any unconscious biases you see today:

How might the messages have been received with a differ-ent frame?

Day 4: Emotional Control

SUBORDINATES

If you don't have anyone that reports to you, you can still do this exercise by practicing this on others at work.

If you *do* have subordinates, the next time you have to have a difficult conversation, practice the Six Steps of Emotional Control.

1. Step back and focus on the other person's emotions.
2. Then look to find the source of the emotions. Does it come from different frames or filters?
3. Talk about feelings openly.
4. Express feelings in a nonconfrontational way.
5. Validate the other person's feelings.
6. Step out of the room if need be.

Describe the experience.

Day 5: Seven Types of Listeners at Work

For each of the following seven types of listeners, identify someone at work who has that predominant style.

The "Preoccupieds"

The "Out-to-Lunchers"

The "Interrupters"

The "Whatevers"

The "Combatives"

The "Analysts"

The "Engagers"

Now, for each person on the list, how will you listen to them more effectively?

Day 6: Decision Styles

Identify people at work whose primary decision styles are the following:

Hierarchic. People who make careful and slow decisions based on a lot of information and analysis.

Integrative. People who use a lot of information and are happy to consider a lot of options.

Decisive. People who use a minimum amount of information to quickly come to clear decisions about a course of action.

Flexible. People who have very fluid thinking styles, using a small amount of information in a lot of different ways.

Day 7: Conflict in the Workplace

The next time you experience conflict at work, practice using the three phases of conflict resolution. Write down your experiences in each phase.

Whom was the conflict with?

What was it about?

Phase One: Explore the other person's viewpoint.
Their view:

Phase Two: Explain your viewpoint.
Your view:

Phase Three: Create resolutions.
Resolutions:

Week Two: Better Listening at Home: Partners, Parents, Siblings, Children, Friends*

Day 8: Response Generators

We'll start our week at home by practicing the response generators. Today, with the people in your personal life, ask them the following questions and see if it elicits a different response than you usually get.

- Oh?
- In what way?
- How so?
- Tell me more . . .
- Give me an example . . .

Describe your results in the following space.

---

* Some of the exercises are adapted from Hearing Resources Center of San Mateo, "Listening Exercises to Help You Be a Better Communicator"; http://www.hearing resourcecentersm.com/ListeningExercisesToHelpYouBecomeaBetterCommunicator. htm; accessed Aug. 19, 2016.

Day 9: Conflict Styles at Home

For each of the following conflict styles, identify the people in your life who demonstrate each style.

The Lion. This style is competitive. They value "winning the point" more than the relationship. They see conflict as a competition. "I know they'll come around once they see my point." It's an "I win/you lose" position.

The Ostrich. This style avoids conflict at all costs. To them, having conflict IS the problem, and it's not worth the trouble to argue because it won't affect the outcome anyway. "I'd rather just forget it." This is a "I lose/you lose" position.

The Dog. This style values the relationship above all else and will accommodate to the other person's desires for the sake of maintaining the relationship. It's the exact opposite of The Lion. "Fine, we'll just do it your way." It's an "I lose/you win" approach.

The Fish. Like a school of fish, this style focuses on collaboration and working together. They want to explore the different options to come up with one where everyone benefits. It's an "I win/you win" approach.

By identifying the styles that the other people are expressing, we are better able to step outside our own frames and into the frame of the other person.

The next few days are going to have you engaging in some fun exercises to help you become a better listener.

Day 10: The Sounds Exercise

Today is all about nonverbal listening. Listen to all sounds around you: a refrigerator humming, a keyboard clicking, an air conditioning system rumbling. Listen to the distant (and not so distant) traffic noise; any airplanes flying by? Listen to people working, people hammering, people mowing the lawn. Listen to people talking, laughing, or crying. Listen to your own noises, your own breathing. What is the "vibe" around you?

Day 11: The Colors Exercise

This is a fun one to do with children. Sit face to face with your child. Tell your child to say a color, such as "red." You respond: "red." Your child says another color: "blue." You respond: "blue." Each time you respond back with the color your child said.

Increase the speed at which you respond to your child. As soon as she starts to say a color, you respond until you are almost saying the colors at the same time.

By the end of the exercise, you and your child will probably be saying colors at the same time! Are you mind reading? No, you are becoming more subtly tuned to listening for their cues because you are focusing more.

Day 12: Charades

This can be played with a group of friends or with your family. Before playing, on index cards, write down some situations and actions. For example, "ordering peanuts at a baseball game."

Teams of two each choose one index card. One person must get his or her partner to guess what he or she is acting out without using words at all.

This helps with listening skills because it requires focus on nonverbal body language.

Day 13: Sympathetic Disagreement

This exercise can be used with a partner or spouse. One person makes a statement. Then the second person repeats what their partner just said that that they agree with, and then politely objects to one specific part of it. For example:

Larry: I love chocolate donuts.

Michelle: I love chocolate donuts, but they are really fattening.

The purpose of this exercise is to practice listening during disagreement.

Day 14: It's a Wrap

Congratulations! You made it to the end of the two weeks. Take some time today to debrief.

What was your favorite exercise?

Do you feel your listening skills have improved?

What things do you think you will continue doing?

Has anyone else made any comments or observations?

Were any of the exercises unsuccessful? What happened?

What was your greatest takeaway from the two weeks?

INDEX